H
069.1
MUS

C0-FSM-398

Monographs on education

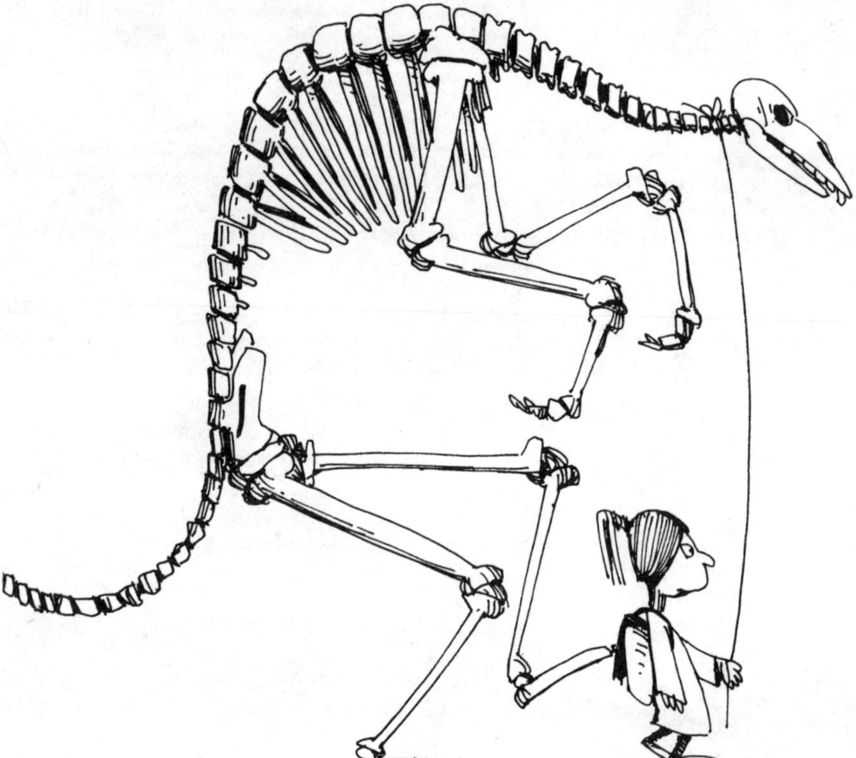

Museums and children

Ulla Keding Olofsson
General Editor

Illustrations
Gerard Teichert

unesco

Published in 1979 by the United Nations
Educational, Scientific and Cultural Organization
7 Place de Fontenoy, 75700 Paris
Printed by Etienne Julien, Paris

ISBN 92-3-101692-X

© Unesco 1979
Printed in France

Preface

1979 is the International Year of the Child and it seems appropriate that the United Nations Educational, Scientific and Cultural Organization (Unesco) should publish *Museums and Children* at this juncture.

Inspiration for this work on the use of museums as educational instruments came from recommendations made by the Conference on the Role of Aesthetic Education in General Education, held at Unesco in December 1974, by two Unesco regional conferences of Ministers of Education (Lagos, 1976 ; Colombo, 1978) and by Unesco regional conferences of Ministers on cultural policies held throughout the 1970s (Venice, 1970 ; Helsinki, 1972 ; Jogjakarta, 1973 ; Accra, 1975 ; and Bogotá, 1978). These recommendations stressed inter alia the advisability of encouraging closer collaboration between schools and cultural bodies, of linking the content of teaching curricula to the cultural heritage of the country and of extending the use of museum resources in education.

One of the aims of education today is to build up learning situations within the community, and museums have an extremely important role in this process. Among the community's most important cultural resources, they allow an interdisciplinary approach to learning and, in fact, constitute laboratories in which teachers and museum personnel can help young people relive vital experiences.

Unesco decided to analyse the role museums do, can and should play as out-of-school educational instruments and to look into their educational activities which are complementary to school programmes. Although this inquiry took place within the framework of Unesco's programme on aesthetic education, its scope was considerably broader, involving many disciplines and various types of museums, ranging from art, history and literature museums to those concerned with natural sciences and even sport.

The task was entrusted to Ulla Keding Olofsson of the Executive Council of the International Council of Museums (ICOM). She assembled fourteen country studies written by museum education specialists throughout the world. Each contributor considered and discussed the themes most relevant to his or her own country and a panoramic view was thereby produced of the situation of museums within differing social, political, economic and cultural contexts.

It is hoped that this work will be instrumental in the transformation of museums into places whose activities complement school programmes by making education personnel aware of both the museum's educational potential and its cultural potential for developing in students a deeper sense of their national heritage, thereby strengthening their cultural identity. Thus it is intended for curricula specialists, educational reformers, museum educators, and schoolteachers. A useful follow-up could involve an exchange of ideas with teachers and those responsible for curricula development in order to analyse school programmes and ascertain the difficulties involved in increased collaboration between schools and museums.

Unesco wishes to express its gratitude to ICOM and its Secretary General, Louis Monreal, without whose encouragement and assistance this work could not have been completed, and to Riksutställningar (Swedish Travelling Exhibitions) for their invaluable aid. Nevertheless, the choice and presentation of facts and the opinions expressed in the following pages are those of the editor and authors; they are not necessarily those of Unesco and do not commit the Organization. The designations employed and the presentation of the material in this work do not imply the expression of any opinion whatsoever on the part of Unesco concerning the legal status of any country or territory or of its authorities, or concerning the delimitations of its frontiers or boundaries.

Contents

Editor's note

The purpose of international co-operation in the field of museum education must be to keep channels open for a steady flow of information, to give professionals opportunities to meet, exchange experiences and be inspired and to support colleagues in museums and in countries where museum education activities have a low priority.

When I was asked to be the editor of a Unesco study on museums as an out-of-school activity, I wanted to give a rich collection of examples of the different ways in which museums are used as educational resources, according to the financial, political, geographical, cultural and educational situations in different countries. At the same time, I wanted to find a way of drawing some conclusions and making some recommendations which could be useful in an international context. I have therefore tried to make this study a team-work effort, and I hope this is reflected in the final version, in spite of its limitations. An important element in the team-work involved in this study was an editorial meeting held in Paris and attended by many of the contributors.

Thanks to a very good response from ICOM members, the main part of this study consists of descriptions of the museum education situation in some countries, selected to present varying situations in different parts of the world. They are not intended as examples to be copied, but rather as illustrations of different methods of tackling a given situation.

Hopefully in the future museums' 'customers', in this case pupils and teachers, will become more involved in the process. Museums all over the world are prepared to play their new role as educational instruments - but are the educational institutions ready to use these instruments? That is a question requiring further investigation.

Introduction

Ulla Keding Olofsson

The most recent assessment of educational activities in museums today is to be found in a work by Kenneth Hudson (43)* in which he summarizes present museum development by saying that museums throughout the world are coming to regard themselves less and less as self-contained professional units and more and more as cultural centres for the communities within which they operate. Museums are no longer considered to be merely storehouses or agents for the preservation

---

* The figures in parentheses throughout the text refer to entries in the Select Bibliography at the end of this publication.

of a country s cultural heritage, but rather as powerful instruments of education in the broadest sense.

The museum as a powerful instrument of education has been a recurrent theme during the last decade not only in museum literature, but also at international museum conferences. The ninth General Conference of the International Council of Museums ICOM held in Paris and Grenoble in 1971, made an important contribution (45). Its International Committee for Education and Cultural Action (CECA) organizes annual conferences on different aspects of museum education. The CECA Conference held in Northern Sweden in 1976 dealt with the roles of regional museums (48,49,91).

Educational activities have, generally speaking, been given a high priority in museums during the 1970s - but it hasn't always been so. For a long time, those working in the museum education field had to fight with colleagues within the museums who regarded other museum activities as more essential: to collect, to preserve, and to carry out research (74).

Attitudes to the different roles of museums also changed outside the museums during the 1970s. When Unesco's periodical *Museum* published a very ambitious special number on Museums and education in 1968, an English Professor of History, John Hale, was asked to write about museums and the teaching of history. He put forward some very progressive ideas regarding exhibition techniques in connection with presentation of historical events, but he opened his article thus:

> 'Let me say at once that I hate the idea of museums being used primarily as teaching aids of any sort. Their first job is to house valuable objects safely and display them attractively.... The second responsibility is to those who already are educated, to the student, the collector, the informed amateur.... A third responsibility to put above anything specifically educational is, in the case of certain museums, a loyalty to their own personalities.' (36)

It would be very difficult to find somebody, inside or outside a museum today, prepared to express such inopportune views.

But museum educators still have problems to fight. At the same time as they are experiencing a growing recognition of their work, they are becoming more aware of a crucial problem - the insufficient contacts with the school system, the main recipient of their services. Lack of interest from teachers, lack of support and confidence from education authorities are recurring complaints. The situation seems to be worse in countries where education and culture are administered from different ministries.

With this situation in view, it is very valuable that Unesco has taken this initiative to make a study on museums as out-of-school activity. Hopefully this study will serve as a starting point for discussions with teachers and others active in the field of education on questions like: 'How can the contacts between museums and schools be improved? How can the educational potentials of museums be better used, taking new educational methods into account?' The discussion of museum education matters on the international level has so far mainly been going on between museum professionals, within ICOM. Perhaps it is time for ICOM to get into contact with other non-governmental organizations to discuss and develop the museum's educational work not only with schools, but also with adult education groups, theatres, libraries and mass media.

The present work will try to describe some general trends within museum education today, the programmes and activities offered, the roles of museum staff and school teachers and some problems in the museum education field, as they are felt in different parts of the world. In various articles there are proposals for a better co-operation between museums and educational institutions and for a better use of museum resources in teaching on all levels.

Much has been written about museums and education - in fact the largest amount of literature on museums concerns education and communication methods (Varine-Bohan, Museum, *The New Encyclopaedia Britannica,* 1974). The Select Bibliography includes books on museums and education in general, from the international point of view such as the already classical *Museums, in search of a usable future* (132), *How to visit a museum* (18) already somewhat old-fashioned when it appeared, and *Museums, imagination and education,* a collection of essays on different aspects of museum education, such as children and art, television, the exhibitions needed in a developing country and travelling exhibitions (123).

Another category of books covered are those presenting museum education resources within one country. Often in the form of a handbook for teachers such as *Pterodactyls and old lace. Museums in education* (103), *Schatzkammer aufschliessen* (94), *Wir besuchen ein Museum* (95) and *Methoden und Medien der Museumsarbeit* (107). The Schools Council in London has also covered an aspect that might lie behind some teachers' hesitant attitude to museums as educational instruments (93).

Most of the titles in the bibliography, however, refer to articles in periodicals. *Museum News*, published by the American Association of Museums (AAM), has run a series of very valuable articles on museum education during the 1970s (partly sponsored by grants from the Smithsonian Institution). Unesco's *Museum* regularly contains contributions on museum education work in different countries (58). The main periodical for museum education internationally is *ICOM Education* (former *Museums' Annual)*, published by CECA. It intends to be a forum for presenting experiences gained in different countries in museums of various types and sizes.

From this Select Bibliography of museum education literature since 1970, it is possible to distinguish some of the general trends in this field at least in Western Europe and North America. To collect information also from other parts of the world, some twenty members of ICOM and CECA, well acquainted with museum education work in their own countries, chosen so as to represent different regions of the world as well as different kinds of museums, were asked for contributions. They received general guidelines indicating more or less the kind of information needed for the study. The request for contributions was sent out in February 1977 and received a very quick and favourable reply. Apparently some of the colleagues had felt a need to summarize their experiences for some time, and they took this opportunity to do so.

Victoria Airey's contribution on Museum Education in the *United Kingdom of Great Britain and Northern Ireland* is an extremely valuable survey of the situation in a country where these activities have very long traditions. I specially want to point out her remark that since the 1960s, museum education officers have had a much wider role in developing and contributing toward adult education and the educational potential of the museum as a whole, as well as their traditional role of museum school officers.

The introductory chapter from Bonnie Pitman-Gelles

forthcoming book on youth education in museums in the *United States of America* also builds on very thorough knowledge about the situation in a whole country, anther country with very well established museum education traditions. Her book will be an important source of ideas and inspiration for museum educators also in other countries.

In *Canada,* Maureen Gee sent out a questionnaire to get the information she needed for her contribution and is building on 100 replies. Her general impression is that 'museum education in Canada today is on a very exciting path'. But she finds that there is a need for more training and more research, and that there is still room for innovation.

Carmo Campos, *Portugal,* also carried out a survey. The answers merely confirmed what she already knew - that the activities of a museum depend wholly on the mentality of the museum director. She summarizes the deficiences she finds in the museum development in her own country as lack of co-ordination, amateurism and a perpetuation of experiments. Museum education services are still regarded as 'poor relatives' in Portugese museums.

Thérèse Destrée-Heymans, *Belgium,* refers to a programme of action for a new museum policy published by the Belgian Museum Association in 1975. In 1971, this Association set up a committee for education and cultural action in Belgian museums which has since made a survey of existing museum education services in the country. It found that, in the majority of Belgian museums, the director has to take care of all the educational activities himself, since he is the only person working full-time in the museum. In the Royal Museum of Art and History in Brussels however, an education service was started as early as 1922 with a staff of its own.

Manfred Kahler, *German Democratic Republic,* describes the education work within a special group of museums, the literature museums in Weimar. Together with a scientific library, memorial sites, large parks and gardens and a Goethe-and-Schiller Archive, they form the *Nationale Forschungs-und Gedenkstätten der klassischen deutschen Literatur in Weimar** which receive one million visitors a year, school groups from all over the country as well as adult groups. Teacher training has a high priority

* National research and memorial centres for German classical literature in Weimar.

in Weimar, and 300-400 teachers go there every year to attend courses lasting a whole week.

The contribution from the *Union of Soviet Socialist Republics*, by V. Tyazhelov, L. Novogilova, V. Dobrovolskaia and I. Kouréeva, describes experiences in three art museums where, for many years, creative activities for different age groups of children have been organized, sometimes integrated with theatre performances. A considerable amount of sociological and psychological research is carried out.

Some of those who had promised to write contributions were unfortunately unable to do so, including two from *Asia*. Therefore, I want to refer to a recent report by Grace Morley, then head of ICOM Regional Agency in Asia, in which she comments that museum education

> 'is an area of modern museum practice that, except in Japan, lags behind Asian museum progress in general. In spite of a few developments that stand out... Asian museums generally restrict their efforts to the long familiar school visit and 'guided lecture tours' of the exhibition galleries The outstanding exceptions of well developed educational services of many types are in the science and technological museums of India - the Birla Industrial and Technological Museum, Calcutta, and the Visvesvaraya Industrial and Technological Museum, Bangalore, which at present not only provide demonstrations for students in the museum's lecture halls, but go to the schools in their home cities, and have groups of teachers for training in science teaching. They also operate extremely valuable mobile museums on trailers, which carry their exhibitions on such themes as 'Power', 'Water; the Fountain of Life', 'Man Must Measure' to rural centres and villages within a 500 or 600 kilometres' radius of the city. It is interesting that some 'cultural' museums in India have followed this example to the extent of equipping trailers or buses with suitable exhibitions, which go to distant quarters of such immense cities as Calcutta and New Delhi (Indian Museum, Calcutta; National Museum and National Gallery of Modern Art, New Delhi), and provide centres of instruction, especially for teachers and for the less favoured segments of the community. Some other Asian countries, especially those

with large village populations, are planning to undertake similar extension services. (83)

There is a contribution from *Thailand,* however, by Chira Chongkol who reports that the Bangkok National Museum has been providing educational services for a long time. In 1969, an education staff was established, now consisting of seven persons. Programmes have been developed for all age groups, and there is a special programme for foreign visitors carried out by a group of volunteers, in English, French, German and Japanese.

In a report from *Iran,* Marie Shaibaie points out that her country is in a state of rapid progress. They are trying to find ways and means suitable for their own national culture and there are plans to establish regional museums. For the moment, a programme with a mobile museum, a bus with a staff of six persons, is going on in regions far away from the capital.

There are four contributions from *Africa.* Emmanuel Arinze, reports that in *Nigeria* the Educational Wing of the National Museum in Lagos is faced with an increase in the demand for educational facilities. The museum has established a 'Communication Channel' with the schools in the Lagos area on an experimental basis, maintaining regular contacts with teachers and sending museum specimens to schools on demand.

The situation looks less favourable in other African countries. The special conditions in the former colonies are vividly described by M'hamed Aït-Djafer, head of an open-air school in *Algeria.* The pre-colonial Algerian museums were never intended for educational purposes. After the independence in 1962, some years passed before anything happened. In 1967, a *Service Educatif des Musées* was created and Aït-Djafer was asked to be responsible, exploring the educational possibilities of museums in Algeria. As many other needs within the country's economy are more pressing for the moment, this service was temporarily suspended for some years. However, brave plans are described for the future, including a museum in every village.

Doreen Nteta's experiences in *Botswana* are similar: museums have to compete with other programmes which are important in the development of a young nation, and they are therefore often given a very low priority. The main problem in her country is that the idea of a 'museum' is new among the indigenous population, and therefore the educational value of the museum is usually overlooked by development planners. In spite of this the National Museum and Art Gallery of Botswana is developing programmes for primary school children, trying to teach environmental conservation and the history of Botswana; in 1977 special programmes also for the Art Gallery were developed.

Oumar Konaré of *Mali*, outlines the situation in a country of 1,220,000 km^2 and 6.3 million inhabitants, with only one museum, the National Museum in Bamako. Like Nteta, he stresses the fact that the museum is not an African institution. The museum, as an institution, like the school, has been mistrusted from the beginning. During the colonial time, the museum expressed foreign ideas and presented African culture only as art, from a folkloric aspect. The museum addressed itself mainly to foreigners, tourists and a national élite. After independence in 1962, a new law on education was passed and a new museum policy was adopted in 1976. Konaré is expecting a change for the better in the future with the museum involved in the general development towards decentralization and democratization in Mali.

Latin America, finally, is represented by *Mexico*. Rodolfo Peltier describes museum education in general, as well as some special projects, such as the *Casa del Museo*, a neighbourhood museum in a slum area in Mexico City, and the school museums, a programme covering around 700 schools for the moment. Museums in Mexico are administered by the Ministry of Education; in a national plan of education under preparation, the use of museums as part of the schools' programmes is being considered. Most museums with more intensive educational activities are found in Mexico City. Peltier's general impression is that the educational resources of Mexican museums are not being used to their full potential.

The fourteen contributions to this study describe, predictibly, very different situations. We find countries in different stages of economic development, countries with dense networks of museums and schools, and countries with just one museum and a school system under construction, countries where reforms of the education system have influenced the pedagogical activities of museums, and countries where present school reforms can be expected to put new demands on the museums' resources.

The widest variety of programmes offered are found in countries with well established museum education services as well as newly reformed school systems, for example in the United Kingdom and the United States. In these countries, museums aim at adopting the latest pedagogical methods by encouraging all kinds of activities involving participation by the pupils. This is done, for example, by special teaching collections, which the pupils are allowed to handle; by demonstrations showing how things work or how things are made, and by role-playing. Such activities are often combined with the use of audio-visual material, such as slides, films, tape recordings, and in the most advanced cases, video-tapes.

However, the most prevalent type of programme, although not usually encouraged by museum educators, is the guided tour of the museum collections. The museums prefer, as Chongkol points out, that classes visit the museum with a specific purpose in mind. But in countries where school classes have to travel a considerable distance to visit the museum, they often want to make the most of their trip and see everything. In a country like Botswana, school children come to the capital Gaborone for a day or two to see everything in town; it may happen that they only have fifteen minutes at their disposal for visiting the Museum and Art Gallery. Since transportation of pupils is very expensive because of the distance, groups can be as large as eighty to one hundred and twenty children. Nteta finds that it isn't possible to do anything for such groups; they are just left to wander about. She finds that the groups have to be restricted to fifteen to twenty pupils to be effectively handled.

In some countries, however, much effort is put into developing the guided tours or gallery talks into meaningful educational experiences. This is the case in U.S.S.R., a fact that has been made clear during two major ICOM conferences held there, in 1968 and in 1977. Museums in U.S.S.R. are extraordinarily well staffed, the Hermitage Museum in Leningrad has ninety museum educators, which explains why this type of staff-consuming museum activity is so much encouraged. In Belgium as well, where museum education services are just starting, guided tours are regarded as very valuable, that is, as Destrée-Heymans points out, provided that the museum visit has been well prepared by the teacher and that the museum educator is able to start a dialogue with the pupils and to adapt the comments to their cultural and social level.

The guided tour is also the main activity of the educational services in museums in Mexico. There it usually begins with an introductory lecture with a film or slide show followed by a visit to one or two rooms or in some cases to an educational exhibition. It can be what is called a Orientation Room, as in the National Museum of Anthropology, with a display of small replicas of archaeological monuments, partly movable, with taped music and comments, or the 'Historical Fact of the Month', as in the National Museum of History, a temporary monthly exhibition with original objects from the museum's collection and an educative interpretation which relates the historical events to the present situation in Mexico. These guided tours end in a workshop where the children make drawings, plasticine models or write essays. In all the tours take from two to four hours and are carried out with groups of thirty to forty pupils.

The *Forschungs- und Gedenkstätten* in Weimar (German Democratic Republic) which receive groups from all over the country recommend the school teachers or group leaders to prepare the excursions before going to Weimar, by using specially designed material comprising slides and travelling exhibitions. The importance of follow-up activities back at home is stressed, and results in the form of essays, drawings, photos, murals and exhibitions are reported.

A tendency in recent years to develop *learning environments,* to emphasize practical work and experiments and drama, to give the pupil an opportunity to examine, study and handle objects is described in the contributions from the United Kingdom and the United States.

Molly Harrison's pioneering ideas at Geffrye Museum in London including allowing children to put on replica costumes to re-enact scenes in period rooms are now generally recognized and have followers, for example in Derbyshire, where a reconstructed chimney allows children to experience the terror of being chimney-sweeping boys. Other day visits include scrubbing floors and laying fires dressed in appropriate costumes.

Pitman-Gelles gives many examples of the special education galleries or discovery rooms which are widely used by science-technology centres and children's museums in the United States. The Exploratorium in San Francisco is described as a library of props where the visitor is allowed to gain first-hand contact with natural phenomena. The Object Gallery of the Florida Isle Museum is designed to complement the exhibitions of the museum and help the visitor to understand the collections' value as teaching and research tools. It contains traditional exhibit cases as well as over 200 drawers of objects. In the Children's Museum of Boston, there are learning environments like Grandmother's Attic and the Japanese Home, where children may dress up, prepare and eat food and sing relevant songs. The new quarters of Brooklyn Children's Museum has incorporated its architecture, its collections, permanent exhibitions, workshop programmes, library and take-home collection into a whole participatory learning environment.

In most countries, guided tours and other kinds of programmes carried out in the museum building can be utilized only by a minority of school classes and other study groups. In some cases, the demand for such museum programmes has to be turned down because of lack of staff, in other cases museums are so far away that transportation becomes an obstacle. Different ways of extending the museum's services beyond the museum walls have consequently been tried out.

In Thailand there are frequent requests from schools which are unable to get to the National Museum in Bangkok. A museum officer may then go to the school to give a talk on a particular subject, using exhibits, photographs, slides or tapes. Canadian national and provincial museums have immense geographic areas for which they are responsible. They send museum educators with travelling museum exhibits to schools sometimes very far away. These programmes are reported to be extremely well received, but they are still rather limited, due to the expenses.

Loan services and travelling exhibitions have been an important part of British museum education services for a long period. The Victoria and Albert Museum in London organized its first travelling exhibition as early as 1855. Museum loan services include original material as well as models and replicas - paintings, drawings, prints, reproductions, films, slides, photographs and wallcharts.

The museum is brought to the classroom in the United States in what are called resource units, which are boxes, trunks, suitcases or portable exhibits containing turtles, rabbits, dioramas, African and Indian masks, supplemented by films and teachers' manuals. Many other programmes have been developed to reach those who for different reasons are not able to come to the museum; the Museum of New Mexico brings art works and artists to schools and communities, while the Boston Museum of Transportation has a Stage Wagon with a troupe of professional actors who perform in auditoriums and community centres.

There are plans in Iran to build a network of small regional museums but experiments with a mobile museum are being carried out in the meantime, involving a bus transporting everything from archaeological specimens to films to 400 folding chairs to small, distant places where they organize their exhibitions making use of whatever is available for large groups of school children.

Finally, two new British developments in the use of mobile units are of particular interest. The Commonwealth Institute in London, is commissioned by museums and provincial communities to develop and circulate, participatory exhibitions depicting the cultural life of a particular commonwealth country in order to further understanding and appreciation of the life and culture of immigrant communities and to help to integrate immigrant and local populations. The other is a mobile van exhibition unit set up in Warwickshire to encourage local communities to investigate into the local environment and to provide educational material for local schools.

The National Institute of Anthropology and History in Mexico has gone a step further in bringing the museum's resources to the schools. It has started a school museum programme involving some 700 schools. Committees consisting of five pupils, two teachers and two parents are responsible for creating and organizing school museums, which are installed in empty rooms in school buildings. The pupils ask the community for material such as wood for showcases and objects to be exhibited; collect minerals, plants and animals, archaeological and ethnographical material, paintings and old photographs; interview people in the community about local traditions; and exchange objects and information with other school museums. A small group of people at the National Institute of Anthropology and History in Mexico City is giving specialized support in regarding anthropology, history and museology while sixty cultural promotion officers handle the programme.

The National Institute of Anthropology and History in Mexico City has also set up a programme for bringing the museum's resources to the groups of the adult population who, for different reasons, never go to the

National Museum of Anthropology, in a neighbourhood museum, *Casa del Museo,* located in a slum area of Mexico City. The aim is to show how the history and culture of Mexico relate to the inhabitants own situation, to help them understand their own problems and to find solutions. The people in the area help work out the exhibitions and activities.

In the last two examples, professional museum staff co-operates with their public - students, teachers, parents, and the local population - in organizing exhibitions and programmes. However, this kind of co-operation is far from being the rule in the organization of educational activities in museums.

Most of the contributors to this study simple did not reply to the question 'In which ways are school authorities, teachers and students involved in the planning and carrying-out of the museum's educational activities?'

According to Peltier, however, 'School teachers have no role in planning museums' educational activities.... there is no permanent contact or link between the museum and local schools, and no consultant or planning group exists. Arinze confesses that co-operation with schools has been a serious problem for some time, but says that there is a marked improvement: museums have always initiated the various programmes, but schools have started to suggest programmes to the museums.

Co-operation between museums and schools in the United States has by tradition been working well on the local level. For some years now, museums have been regarded, in the legal sense, as 'educational institutions'. This has resulted in a flow of federal funds to museums and schools for curriculum development projects to be carried out in co-operation, i.e. at the Lawrence Hall of Science, curricula in computer education are developed for deaf adults, language and arts for American Indian children and science enrichment activities for the visually handicapped.

Most of the contributors to this study report that their museums co-operate with schools and teacher training colleges in training teachers how to use the museum's resources. Training classroom teachers how to use museums effectively is felt to be very important, not only because the classroom teacher knows the pupils and the curriculum best, but also because demand for museum education programmes is outstripping the museum staff capacity. But there is much to be done when it comes to the training of the museums' educational staff. The lack of training for museum educators in most countries has been a matter for concern and discussion at international conferences for many years. In most cases the training takes the form of on-the-job training. Whether a teacher with further training in the museum disciplines or a curator with further training in education becomes the better museum educator is another eternal matter for discussion at museum education conferences.

There are few examples of museum education activities being planned and carried out in co-operation with other museums or in co-operation with other institutions such as theatres, libraries, television companies, etc. Some attempts at inter-museum co-operation in the United Kingdom are described, one of which involved the Geffrye Museum, the National Army Museum and the National Portrait Gallery working together on different aspects of the Civil Wars. They co-operated with a travelling theatre group to dramatize incidents, to make television programmes and to help schools recreate the period and its events.

The National Museum of Thailand and the National Theatre are co-operating on a pilot project on Museums and Adult Education and activities involve travelling exhibitions by day and dancing and music by night. In the United States there are examples from Cleveland and Oakland of collaborative projects where all the cultural resources in a community are integrated. If the theme of study is African art or the history of the court system, the students visit the zoo, the court house, the art museum, the historical society and other relevant institutions.

Fieldwork in connection with museum visits is reported from Mexico, the United States and the United Kingdom generally in the form of activities offered to children during weekends and holidays, organized as street trails or town trails in the local area or as excursions to collect specimens or to study archaeological excavations.

In Algeria, museums co-operate regularly with *La Télévision Algérienne* in producing and broadcasting television programmes intended to make a new and broad public acquainted with the resources of Algerian museums.

The Alaska State Museum in the United States develops education programmes which are broadcast throughout the state on the educational television network.

A trend towards a closer, more integrated co-operation

between museums and other institutions and groups in society can be noticed, however, specially on regional and local levels. The British system of Local Education Authorities, involves a number of support services including a Schools Library Service, Technology Resource Centre, Schools Health Service, Schools Art Service and a Schools Museum Service. In addition schools can expect support from the Forestry Commission, the Nature Conservancy Council, the National Trust, Archives Offices, Naturalist's Trust, the Directorate of Ancient Monuments and Historic Buildings of the Department of the Environment, etc. It is therefore common practice for a museum education officer to be in touch with all such relevant organizations in an area, to give or receive help, *to pool available resources*.

Other examples of such pooling of resources are found in the literature listed in the Select Bibliography such as the Museums Collaborative (8) a group established in 1970 by New York City's Department of Cultural Affairs for two purposes to decentralize museum resources and to use them in 'new ways with new audiences' and to ease some of the tasks of museum education departments through such collective services as joint fund-raising and information exchange. The organization has a full-time staff of five. Twenty-five cultural institutions are members, and museums, schools and the business community are represented on the board of trustees. The programme includes setting up permanent cultural resource centres, directly related to the school curriculum and maintained by the schools to provide places for museum resources, local community artists, and school needs to come together free from the constraints of museum and classroom.

A somewhat similar method for pooling of resources is being used in Sweden, where the Government set up an experimental organization in 1965, *Riksutställningar* (Swedish Travelling Exhibitions), which has been working as a permanent institution with a staff of sixty since 1976 (4,43,90).

Riksutställningar aims include finding new and imaginative ways for the use of exhibitions in education on all levels, by co-operating with museums, schools, adult education groups, libraries, designers, artists - with all those who can contribute to the development by their special experience or knowledge. Among the co-operative experiments going on at

Riksutställningar is the development of small, portable exhibitions, so-called *kits*.

The pooling of resources found in museums, schools, libraries and archives by making-up small teaching packages, portable exhibitions, 'kits', has often been reported during museum conferences. During the 1971 ICOM conference in France, a working party was set up within the Education Committee to collect and distribute information regarding such projects, and to promote international co-operation in the production and exchange of kits. As a first result, the Working Party on kits published a simple, illustrated booklet (47) giving a short definition and description of what a good kit ought to be:

> 'In the field of the museums and cultural institutions the kit design is a portable unit suitable for serial production which is available for hire or sale.
>
> 'This unit follows special aims regarding instruction and education and is suitable particularly to stimulate individual and collective self activity.
>
> 'The elements of the unit are compiled in accordance with a clearly defined theme. Special care is given to the integration of the different elements of the unit.
>
> 'The selection of the theme and the elements of each unit is a co-operative effort of museums, pedagogic and other specialists with regard to the requirements of known or potential users.
>
> 'Prior to serial production each unit undergoes a test on its different possibilities.
>
> 'A kit may comprise:
>
> a) original material,
> b) corresponding forms of representation, such as replicas, facsimiles, reproductions and models,
> c) audio-visual media, such as records, tapes, slides, films, video-records, video-cassettes etc.,
> d) supplementary material such as maps, diagrams, drawings, photographs, etc.,
> e) expendable material such as work sheets, specially designed for those who use it,
> f) suggestions for the didactical and methodical as well as the practical use of the unit.

'For storage and transport, the elements of the unit are packed in a handy, protective case, which may be used in presentation.
'For administration, control and evaluation of the use of the unit it is necessary to develop a suitable system.'

Algeria

M'Hamed Aït-Djafer

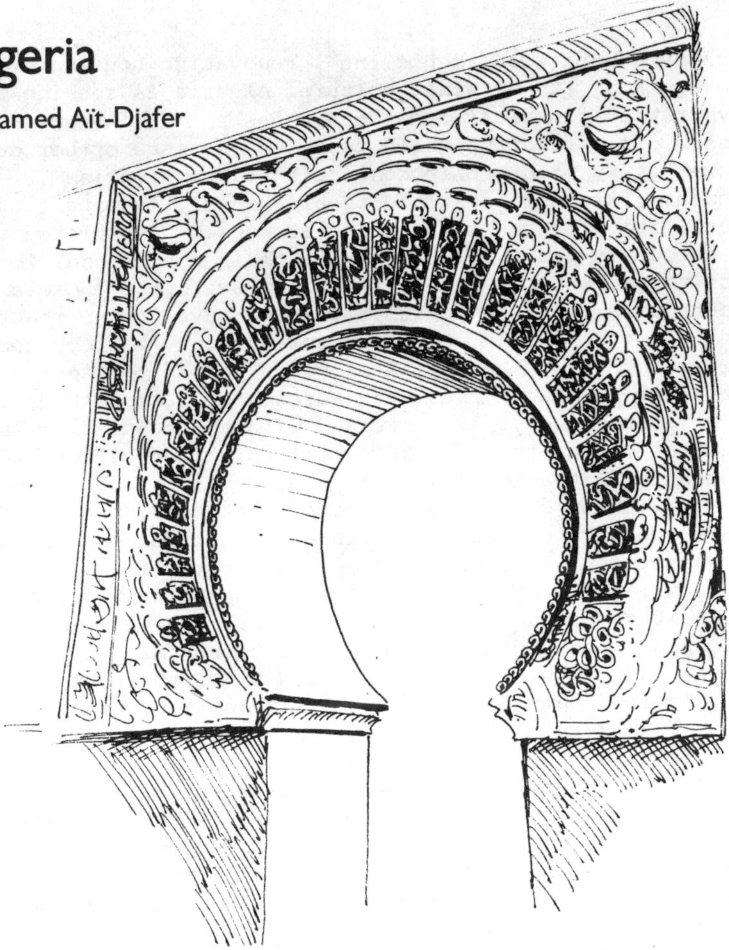

Algeria has only just emerged from a long nightmare which began in 1830 with the French Conquest and the ensuing gradual decay of its own culture and which ended in a bloodbath, from 1954 to 1962, the war of liberation, which resulted in independence at the price of one and a half million dead and the almost complete destruction of the country's material and economic infrastructure.

Even now, after a decade and a half of heroic labour, Algeria has not yet finished dressing its wounds and strenuous efforts are still required to solve all kinds of problems, whether they concern constructing a modern economy, modernizing agriculture, achieving universal schooling*, renovating housing or reacquiring its original culture. Algeria is seeking to syncretize classical humanist values and the Arabo-Islamic civilization which forms the essence of her culture. It is within this context that the Algerian museums, although destined to play a very important cultural role for the future, are at present restricted to a secondary position. Similarly, their educational role for the moment is seen in terms of developing those aspects of Arabo-Islamic culture which have lain dormant, largely ignored and forgotten for so long, thereby contributing to awakening the Algerian people to their cultural heritage. Thus, the Museums Educational Service, a government body, is concerned with the population in general rather than the more limited milieu of formal education - teachers, schools and school children.

The museum's most important task at present is to pave the way for optimum cultural effectiveness, by means of realistic projects such as : creating new museums; training a specialized personnel taking into account future demands, which entails flexible systematic planning; and making the population aware of this, their own culture, a culture which is virtually unknown particularly among schools and universities, youth movements, workers' and women's movements as well as rural movements.

Therefore, this study, will deal with the problems of regaining through the intermediary of existing or new museums, the Arabo-Islamic personality of the Algerian people and of finding its place in the modern world in order to participate in 'enrichment through mutual differences'.

The programmes and activities, generally offered to adults, mainly deal with the archeological sites of the Roman Culture the (first to fifth Centuries A.D.), of the Catholic implantation towards the fourth Century (St. Augustine, etc.) but they ignore the Arabo-Islamic civilizing mission.

As well as the famous historical sites such as Timgad,

---

* Over one million children between the ages of 6 and 14 do not attend school. At present, 72 per cent of children attend school, compared with about 10 per cent in 1962, at which time 100 per cent of European children went to school. (Statistics provided by the Ministry of Education)

Djemila, Tipasa, Cherchell, Hippone etc., other museums none the less gave nodding recognition to Arabic Civilization, for example, the Museum of Antiquities in Algiers, and the multidisciplinary local museums of Oran and Constantine with their remarkable collections of paintings and sculpture. In these three museums, one can find traces of the brilliant civilization of the Rostomids (ninth to eleventh centuries), the Hammadites (eleventh century) and even a few more recent objects of the Turkish period (sixteenth to eighteenth centuries).

The Bardo Prehistory and Ethnography Museum (Algiers) and the National Fine Arts Museum (Algiers) with their very beautiful collections of paintings and sculptures of the fifteenth to twentieth centuries, warrant comparison with similar museums anywhere.

Lastly, numerous Natural Science sections (particularly in Oran, Constantine, Bousmaïl, Bedjaïa and Beni-Abbes) and an excellent Botanical Museum (Nursery Garden in Algiers) were created by the French.

Up to now, in organizing museums; children's educational needs were in no way taken into account everything was reserved for adults.

After Algeria's independence, the status quo remained for several years, and there was fortunately no widespread destruction. Although just before independence France had 'repatriated' the collections of the large *Franchet d'Espérey* Museum (Algiers), and the most important treasures from the collections of paintings of different periods from the National Fine Arts Museum; the latter were restored after negotiations.

In 1967, Algeria received donations from friendly nations (dolls, collections of costumes, stamps, model aeroplanes, prints etc.) which inspired the creation of a 'Children's Museum' in Algiers, and a year later a 'Museums Educational Service' attached to the Ministry of Education. The Museums Educational Service, had a very precise task : to exploit all the educational and training possibilities of Algerian museums for the benefit of children and adolescents.

As far as schools were concerned, these possibilities lay mainly in the realm of history and the natural sciences (at the primary and middle school levels), as well as prehistory, the arts, ethnography and handicrafts (at the secondary and higher levels).

The Museums Educational Service undertook a vast information campaign for the teaching profession leading to concrete educational action within schools and universities : organizing training courses for teachers and guided and lecture tours for pupils and students, encouraging visits to the museum and organizing numerous exhibitions of children's drawings, various competitions with prizes, etc.

At the same time, steps were taken to make museum technicians, more aware of the cultural and educational functions that museums should have in addition to their traditional functions of conservation, exhibition and scientific research. This was based mainly on practical work and lectures, and efforts were made to train experienced guides amongst the museum guards.

Since 1971, after passing through several administrative reorganizations, museums became the responsibility of the Ministry of Information and Culture and the administrative infrastructure of cultural affaires in general was reinforced. It is gratifying that deliberate efforts have been made to do the utmost to preserve the museological, archaeological and historical heritage and to put it to renewed educational and cultural use by launching a programme for the construction of new museums and by infusing life into a Museums Educational Service which during the preceding years had been virtually inactive.

It is true that only the schools and university level establishments which are motivated continue to make use of the possibilities offered by museum visits, and the guard-guides, little interested by an increase in their work-load, are all too happy to remain simply guards. However, some guards who have followed courses, continue to give explanations to those who ask for them, and as there seems to exist an increasing desire to remedy the present situation, one can only be optimistic as to the educational and cultural future of the Algerian museums.

*Aims and methods of museums's educational work**

Didactic. For children and adolescents attending school or members of youth movements, as part of their research projects, talks were given to their class or group; the main fields of interest here were in history, prehistory,

* I shall deal here only with activities sponsored by the Museums Educational Service from 1967 to 1970, when I was in charge of it (author's note).

science (especially natural science) and, at the university level the arts (especially visual arts).

Leisure. Guided visit days to museums, archaeological sites and monuments were organized for all types of public (children, family associations, trade union members, etc.).

Aesthetic education. Especially for the young, guided visits to art galleries, local handicraft museums and mosques characteristic of the different periods of Arabic civilization (tenth to eighteenth centuries) were organized.

Guided visits and lecture tours of sites and monuments were specially organized in order to give teachers some training, so as to encourage them to train others in turn. This was followed by practical training in the form of guided visits with classes. Two examples follow.

A visit to the Children's Museum in Algiers involved a group of twenty children accompanied by ten trainee-teachers. In each of the six rooms (exhibition of children's drawings, eleventh century Muslin architecture, local and foreign costumes, foreign dolls, stamp collections, model aircraft construction and printing), the children first looked around freely, absorbing their surroundings in silence for two or three minutes. This was followed by a short lecture adapted to their level, and lastly, a game of questions and answers with the drawing of sketches or the taking of notes.

On another occasion, a visit to the Roman Ruins of Tipasa (60 km from Algiers) included thirty children and fifteen trainee-teachers. In this particular case, a whole day was needed, as well as organized transport and meals. The number of the participants was probably too large from the educational point of view, but in order to make the operation viable, the forty-five seats in the bus had to be occupied. Upon arrival, first they visited the marvellous little site museum, whose one room has an excellent choice of well exhibited specimens and objects. There also, after a few minutes absorbing their surroundings, a lecture was given mainly in front of the map which showed all the details concerning the ruins, followed by a game of questions and answers with note-taking and sketches. This in turn was followed by a two-hour visit to the site itself (a large Roman town, very complete and well-preserved). Although too brief for the children's taste, this encouraged them to come back again with their parents and friends. The visit ended with a singing session in the Roman Theatre, where children and adults alike take part with great enthusiasm.

After lunch, the group usually returned to Algiers, visiting the imposing and mysterious Royal Tomb of Mauritania (ex-tomb of the Christian Woman, 12 km east of Tipasa) on the way. With their heads full of extraordinary shapes and colours, the children and the trainee-teachers were happy and full of enthusiasm, the latter went on to explore fields which had been completely outside their ken before.

Visits to mosques. Religious Education (Islam) is official in Algeria and is included in the school curricula. This is an excellent opportunity to visit the mosques some of which are real jewels, characteristic of the different Islamic periods. For example, in Algiers there is the Grand Mosque (Ommayad, eleventh century), the *Ketchaoua* mosque of pure Ottoman style (seventeenth century), the new 'modern' Turkish mosque (eighteenth century), not to mention a multitude of small mosques in the Casbah, each one having its own distinctive style and originality. All this priceless heritage is unfortunately not made use of, either on the aesthetic or on the cultural level. Visits were organized to those which differed a little from those to museums in the sense that silence had to be respected in the place of worship. Thus the preparation and follow-up activities, when the public is made up of schoolchildren or undergraduates, are not the same as for visits to museums.

Visit to the Casbah. The Casbah in Algiers is an immense living museum of urbanism and architecture - specifically Turkish, from the sixteenth to eighteenth centuries - and of old and new ethnography; a population of 70,000 inhabitants lives there, certainly under difficult conditions (the population density is one of the highest in the world), but retaining a certain character and specific traditions. All types of public find it a fascinating place to visit. One visit showed architecture students an architecture, particularly well adapted to the population's way of life in the seventeenth and eighteenth centuries as well as especially functional for the period. Indeed the Casbah in Algiers is unique and from all points of view it can be of great benefit to visit it; it is of touristic interest, as well as didactic, historic, cultural, aesthetic and ethnographic interest. Even the children who live there and go to school there were very happy to understand their everyday

environment and to be able to situate it not only as regards its history but also its geography and aesthetics. Their eyes could be seen to shine with the pleasure of 'having understood'.

There are three aspects involved in the preparatory stage for museums' educational work - administrative, technical and material. The first aspect to be considered is *administration* : for all the activities, the authorities concerned have to give their approval, if only as regards the organization and planning (authorities responsible for the museums, sites and monuments, school or university authorities, organization of transport, supervision, etc.). In terms of the *technical* aspects, it is left to the schools to choose the classes that are to participate; in general, the institutions themselves call on the Museums Educational Service which delegates a representative to prepare for the chosen activity by means of lectures illustrated by leaflets, photographs and sketches. The *material* side, preparation of the supervision, transport, food etc., is worked out in liaison with the person in charge of the establishment.

Special activities are usually organized as a reward for the best pupils or the best classes. Anticipation of them, therefore, helps stimulate school work. Planning is done well in advance, particularly for day-trips.

Visits to museums are simpler and usually left to the initiative of the teachers, who merely inform the Museums Educational Service twenty-four hours in advance. Where possible, the Service will delegate a representative to act as guide and lecturer.

Afterwards, follow-up activities involve the young

visitors in sending in the work they have done (essays, drawings, paintings, etc.), through the Head of the establishment and after scrutiny by their teachers. The best are kept and exhibited in the Children's Museum in Algiers. The creation of classroom museums is encouraged in those classes whose pupils have taken part in the museum educational activities: stone and shell collections, herbaria, butterflies, drawings and paintings, reproductions of mosques made solely out of matchsticks and glue, and even a simple but particularly evocative diorama of Tipasa.

Original specimens and objets d'art are jealously guarded by the museums and the only means of using them is to look at them and make sketches (photography being strictly forbidden, unless the Department of Fine Arts makes a special exception to the rule). These precautions are justified at present, for our children (and even some adults) have little respect, mostly out of ignorance, for these objects and specimens which they admire without being clearly aware of their fragile nature and scientific value. The museum personnel's primary task (especially the guards') is to safeguard the objects from damage caused by the public or by humidity, dust etc. Moreover, very clear explanatory notices in Arabic and in French are often hung up and serve as basic documentation.

The Museums Educational Service has undertaken numerous experimental activities, all of which were initially crowned with success, but little has been done to systematize them. Future activities may involve the creation of 'kits' and of museum buses, the organization of temporary exhibitions, etc.

Recently, Algerian Television (in accordance with a suggestion put forward by the Museums Educational Service) has made great efforts to publicize and widen the influence of museums, archaeological sites and historical monuments in the country by producing many excellent films which should certainly incite a considerable public to visit the museums and sites that have been filmed, and even others as well.

As mentioned above, the clearly defined mission of the Museums Educational Service was to make the country's museums, sites and monuments known, as the museum authorities had become aware of the nearly total indifference of the majority of the public (foreign tourists excepted). It became clear very quickly that education had a vital role to play in this process. Thus a series of activities was suggested and approved despite the obvious lack of manpower, equipment and technical and financial resources.

First of all, a complete list of museums (with their fields of specialization and addresses) was compiled by catagory (National Museum, Site Museum, Municipal Museum, etc.). In addition, a complete list of archaeological sites and main historical monuments was made out on the same basis. This first set of documents was distributed in the principal schools and universities with a circular aimed at stimulating their interest and offering to organize guided and lecture visits on request. Lastly, each year courses are organized aimed at stimulating awareness amongst a very specific public: firstly, of course, the museum personnel (technicians, curators, research assistants, guards, etc.); next, teachers from different regions in Algeria. These courses, lasting two weeks, were designed in the following way : one week's practical introduction to museum science (including visits to local museums and monuments); one week's tour of the country, visiting the main museums, sites and monuments, where possible following a given theme (i.e. Rome, Islam, Popular Arts and Traditions, etc.).

In addition, several very short seminars were held for museum curators, chief researchers and archaeologists to draw their attention to the importance of the cultural and educational role of museums and to enlist their active support whenever groups arrive in their institutions. These small seminars brought a breath of fresh air into the museums and were very successful, especially since they also gave the ICOM National Committee an opportunity to speak of its activities and extend its influence among the highly qualified museum personnel.

Monographs by the participants in these seminars have been published, including an excellent study on Tipasa, a catalogue of the National Fine Arts Museum collections as well as those of the Bardo Museum and a study of the Lambèse site and museum. The publication of many other works of this kind, intended mainly for the information and enlightenment of the general public, has been hampered by lack of funds.

But the most enthusiastic of all were those primary and secondary school pupils who had agreed to make up practice classes' for the various courses. The Museums Educational Service was bombarded with their essays, drawings, paintings and even reproductions of objects made out of modelling clay.

The museum staff's role in the educational activities of the museum is almost nonexistent. Only the technicians and curators are directly concerned by their museum's influence. However, their role is a somewhat passive one, limited to welcoming all visiting groups. They do not participate in any kind of planning beforehand.

The heads of the establishments concerned contact either the Museums Educational Service or the museums directly. Each museum compiles statistics on the number and type of groups of visitors.

The educational activities of museums feature in the various curricula for teacher-training courses but they are not obligatory, and are often considered as leisure activities rather than as necessary training. This is due to the accelerated training schemes which have been imposed as a result of the acute teacher shortage. Thus the training of teachers for middle schools lasts eleven months after the *Baccalauréat**, with further in-service training extending over several years.

This leaves much to be desired in a country where many have never heard of a museum. The means employed for informing the general public are unfortunately, therefore, rather limited: a list of the thirty museums with their main characteristics, published by the Museums Educational Service; catalogues of a few museums, published by the museums themselves, with the help of the Department of Fine Arts; reprinting of the excellent works published before Independence on Tipasa, Djemila and Timgad (others, such as one about Cherchell, are out of print); and the publication of new works dealing with the Royal Tomb of Mauritani , the main Algerian museums, the mosques, the Casbah, the Tassili frescoes, a recently discovered hoard of coins, etc.

However, several excellent films about the museums, mosques and archaeological sites, especially Muslim ones (Kalaâ of Beni Hammad, Tlemcen, etc.), have also been made by Algerian Television and greatly contribute to their becoming popular with the general public.

---

* Secondary school graduation diploma

Summary

There are thirty museums in Algeria for a population of more than 18 million inhabitants (1977 census). If we compare this with any country in the socialist or capitalist bloc, or even with some of the Third World countries, the difference is striking. The main causes are probably the following. The museums, established by the occupying power in conformity with its own ethics and the cultural needs of the metropolitan country, affected almost exclusively the European population or 'settlers'.

After Independence, Algeria was faced with a desperate situation on all levels, with an order of urgency which naturally placed, and still does, cultural needs at the bottom of the list, in particular far behind the goal of universal schooling in a country where 60 per cent of the population is under 24 years of age, and which in 1962 had an illiteracy rate of 92 per cent.

Among the primary tasks is naturally that of rebuilding the country, creating a balanced economy such as will redress the colonial heritage (let us remember that Algeria produces between 5 and 10 million hectolitres of wine for a Muslim population to whom wine-drinking is forbidden), creating an independent industry, progressively implementing the country's policy options.

Pushed thus into the background, museums currently are visited mostly by foreign tourists and, since the creation of the Museums Educational Service, by a few schools and universities or youth movements which have been made aware of their cultural and educational aspects. Individuals rarely visit museums of their own volition, despite the adequate publicity they receive through the mass media (for example, the weekly cultural supplement to the daily *El Moudjahid)*.

It must be said that, the small number of museums does not encourage people to visit and almost no effort has been made to build more of them, except for a very serious project which has been under discussion for five years now, to establish a *Moudjahid* Museum (combatants' museum) with a precise and ambitions mission : to reconstruct as fully as possible the painful history of the fight for national independence, in particular from 1954 to 1962. With this in mind, a vast national campaign for the collection of objects, specimens, photographs and documents which belonged to the *maquisards*, or which were used during the struggle for liberation, was launched several years ago and these objects are now being compiled, filed, restored and prepared for the constitution of collections.

It seems unlikely that the museum will be open to the public for several years yet, as there remains so much preparatory work to be completed.

Suggestions for the future

It is possible to create a quantity of new museums, spread throughout the country, within the framework of the accelerated decentralization campaign which the Government is now pursuing. They could include *museums which have already been under study* in depth and which are ready to be created such as the Nasreddine Dinet Museum at Boussada, depicting the work of this early twentieth century French painter who embraced the Islamic religion.

A new idea which appeared in conjunction with the creation of the 'Thousand villages of the Agrarian Revolution', decreed by President Boumedienne in 1972 was the creation of a museum in each village of the Agrarian Revolution. At present, seventy-nine of these villages have been completed and are inhabited and 334 more are being built. It is possible to go more deeply into this idea and adapt it to the educational and cultural needs of the rural population (i.e. agricultural museums).

Another way of developing and enhancing awareness of the Arabo-Islamic archaeological riches dispersed throughout the country, i.e., at Kalaâ of Beni Hammad, Sidi Okba, Miliana, Mansourah, Honaîne, etc. would be through the opening up currently neglected sites and the constructing of small museums on or near them. *Museums of folk art and popular tradition* (similar, for example, to the Ghardaîa Museum of Folklore) could be set up throughout Algeria, based on the immense wealth of traditional handicrafts which are put to virtually no cultural use, rather hiddenaway in almost every town or village. For the last few years, the Algerian authorities have made a great effort to encourage the traditional handicrafts which make up part of authentic folk art, especially in the countryside, and the museums could have a role to play in this campaign. *Technical Museums* are another possibility such as the 'petrol museum' organized each year at the Algiers International Fair by SONATRACH, the National Oil Corporation, as is a *museum of sport,* covering old and new sports. The latter in particular would meet an important need, given young people's often passionate interest in sport.

Educational personnel, technicians, museologists, restorers and guards require specific training which will have to be carried out efficiently and at reasonable cost a possible first step would be the creation of a specialized advisory commission, whose task would be to draw up job descriptions for the various categories of personnel required, and devise the corresponding training programmes.

School exchanges could be organized with a view to making known to the country's young the particularities of each region, by means of its museums, sites and monuments.

Belgium

Thérèse Destrée-Heymans

Education services have officially existed in State Museums in Belgium since 1965, when an increase in staff made it possible for the museums to assign to their Education Services scentific personnel with a career structure similar to that of the curatorial staff. However, at the Royal Museums of Art and History, an Education service had been set up as early as 1922 on the initiative of Chief Curator Capart, an eminent egyptologist and also a convinced believer in the educational role of museums. For forty-three years, this service sought to apply active teaching methods by means of guided visits for schools; it also built up a slide collection which today has more than 40,000 slides and remains a very precious working aid for teachers.

In 1965 no other museum in Belgium allotted such a large staff to its Education Service, that is to say, six people (three Dutch-speaking and three French-speaking).

In the other State Museums, one or two people were permanently attached to the Education Services.

A number of provincial or municipal museums now have an Education Service run as a non-profit-making organization, subsidized by the province or local authorities. In most Belgian Museums, however, the Curator himself is in charge of the educational activities, being in many cases the only full-time member of the museum staff*.

The Association of Belgian Museums has, for its part, clearly shown the importance it attaches to the educational role of museums by setting up in 1971 the *Commission education et action culturelle dans les musées belges***.

Among other activities the Commission has conducted a survey into the functioning of Education Services in State Museums and organized several national one-day seminars.

The Commission's main aim is to foster cultural promotion work in Belgian museums and to establish contacts and exchanges on an international level. In 1973 it defined the tasks of Education Services in State museums and suggested that the Education Service form a department on the same level as those in charge of the curatorial work, and that it should be under the Director's or Chief Curator's direct responsibility.

This education and cultural information department should be composed of the following elements.

The Head of Department is the general co-ordinator and is responsible for everything that has not been assigned to particular sections. He is in charge of the training of the department's personnel as well as the recruiting of temporary staff.

A 'pedagogical and museological' section of which the main tasks consist of: collaboration with the curator and the designer for the didactic presentation

---

* This study was based on a report by the Association of Belgian Museums (5)

** Commission for Educational and Cultural Promotion Work in Belgian Museums.

of the museum's collections; collaborating on the setting up of exhibitions; organizing thematic exhibitions bringing out a particular aspect of the collections; and devising training programmes for teachers and future members of museum education services.

A teaching and lifelong education section whose main task is to contact schools and other educational establishments, at the primary, secondary or higher level, with a view to organizing guided tours, lecture tours or discussion groups. It is also in charge of organizing conferences and lecture tours for the public in general as well as youth activities, workshops, training sessions, etc.

A documentation and information section which would compile and offer to the public general documentation on the museum, make available to the public a media library (slides, films, etc.), prepare explanatory leaflets, organize the reception of visitors and groups and be the information centre for the museum's activities.

This department should be backed up by an administrative section (secretariat, accounting) and by a technical section (draughtsman, designer, photographer and documentalist).

The Commission for Educational and Cultural Promotion Work organized a one-day seminar to discuss the problem of training educational and cultural promotion staff*.

The Education Services in museums at present employ on a free-lance basis university or college graduates paid in fees, without any official employment contract. This is contrary to labour law, and an alternative solution should therefore be found. The present system also impairs the smooth functioning of the Education Service, which has an insufficient number of permanent staff to take on all the educational work on their own. Besides the museum educational staff, there are also cultural promotion staff whose training may differ.

* The mimeographed report of this seminar can be obtained from the Commission itself *(Commission education et action culturelle dans les musées belges)*.

Even though certain museums do not make this distinction, in particular the Fine Arts Museums in Brussels, most of them employ cultural promotion staff, artists, visual arts teachers, art historians, etc. for their creative workshops. In certain cases museum educational and cultural promotion staff work together on the creation of pedagogical programmes. For this purpose they receive extra training, sometimes in the form of a course in the museums, since a diploma for museum educational and cultural promotion staff does not yet exist. It should be emphasized that the specific nature of each museum implies a special pedagogy differing from that applied in the school environment, and that *in situ* training of the teaching staff appears indispensable.

In the Royal Museums of Art and History a subsidy, is granted by the Ministry of French Culture to the expression and creativity workshop, *Dynamusée,* so that it may organize study days and weekend training sessions for cultural promotion staff wishing to specialize in this field.

The programme is composed of, on the one hand, study of the environment (the museum) and its multiple resources, and on the other hand creative expression work in the workshop around a given theme.

The whole operation implies an interdisciplinary approach to the museum objects and the active participation of all the cultural promotion staff. The task of the co-ordinator, a specialized cultural promotion officer, will be to lead the group to give free expression, using one or more expressive techniques (graphic, pictoral, formal, gestural or corporal), to what they have learnt from the study of one or of several objects in the museum.

The *status of the educational and cultural promotion staff* poses a problem which today confronts all the State Museums. During the National Symposium on 'The Museum and Society. Cultural Promotion Work and Museums.', organized by the Commission for Educational and Cultural Promotion Work (8 - 9 December 1977), the necessity of giving such staff official status was widely confirmed.

A working-group is studying the data of the problem, the complexity of which is further aggravated by the present economic crisis. It is nevertheless vital that a solution to it be found so as to ensure the survival of the education services, upon which greater and greater responsibilities are falling, and whose structures are not clearly defined. It should be possible for this problem to be studied on a European level and we sincerely hope that a European Conference may be organized in order to define the status of the staff in question in terms equally applicable to the non-graduate personnel who should be integrated into the Education Services.

One of the primary tasks of any Education Service is to meet the demands of schools wishing to find in the museum the indispensable complement to the school curricula. It is with this aim in mind that the museums, as far as they are able, are trying to find a solution so as to respond in the most adequate way to the needs of schools. The museums offer them a very wide choice of possibilities. The most common is still the guided visit which is purely informative and limited to a very precise historical subject. This is very beneficial if the teacher has prepared his class for it, so that it can stimulate a response and serve as a subject for study back in the schoolroom. The problem facing the person conducting the guided visit is to promote, in the space of an hour, an interest and a dialogue and to adapt his or her commentary to the cultural and social level of the group of pupils. This is a delicate task, requiring a very wide historical and scientific knowledge and a fair amount of psychology and pedagogical experience.

In the last ten years, the school curricula, and mainly those in secondary education, have been largely modified, in what is today called 'renewed' teaching. Apart from the curricula content, the new teaching methods, which require greater student participation, have changed the very conception of the pupil as well as the teachers' need.

This evolution led the Education Services to propose thematic visits with questionnaires, thus allowing greater student participation. Certain visits, so-called *creative visits* lead to practical work in the workshops following a visit to a very limited section, or even one painting or a few exhibits.

The Education Services of all the State Museums responsible to the two Ministries of Culture - the

Royal Fine Arts Museums in Brussels, the Royal Museums of Art and History in Brussels, the Royal Museum of Mariemont, the Fine Arts Museums in Antwerp - have creative workshops in liaison with the museum collections. These creative workshops offer programmes for schools and adult education as well as leisure activities. Their aim is to teach *how to see* and to relive the past creations of mankind within a contemporary context. Thus they favour a greater integration of the individual into his environment. Museum exhibits do in fact favour and spark off creative expression when they are approached from an interdisciplinary point of view. This means that, apart from their historical, artistic or archaeological value, they carry a sociological message, deriving as they do from specific construction techniques linked to particular geographical, economic and social contexts. All this will favour the stimulation of creative expression within the framework of the workshop. It is hoped that this 'cultural promotion' or 'animation' approach, which is a relatively recent feature of museum work, will allow the active and lively role that museums can play in formal education to be better understood. (109)

Another variant which is frequently proposed and adopted by schools is that of introducing the visits to the collections themselves by a talk, illustrated by slides; this introduction can be held at the schools or at the museum itself.

Activities organized outside the museum or the school, in the form of field-excursions, are arranged by the Royal Institute of Natural Science.

Unfortunately, it must be noted that up to the present time, a common programme exploiting possibilities in different types of museums, in order to provide the teacher with a wider choice as to the illustration of a theme or a school subject, has not yet been elaborated.

The school public, that is to say the age of children who most often visit the museums, depends on the type of museum. However, the largest number of guided tours are requested by secondary schools, (pupils from 12 to 18 years of age). Requests from groups of students in higher education are rarer; the latter are in fact shown around the museum by their own teachers in most cases. Children in primary schools (6 to 12 years old) take part more frequently in creative visits. These types of visits allow the child to become familiar with the environment (the museum) to explore it freely and to rediscover the joys of drawing, painting and modelling there. In the first stage the child must have 'enjoyed himself' in the museum in order to be able to 'like it' subsequently.

The colleges that train primary school teachers and those of middle and secondary schools make up an especially important section of the public. They are the ones who will in the future, have to prepare their pupils for museum visits. The Education Services prepare a variety of activities for them in the form of debates or creative work in the workshops. Then there are groups from the specialized schools for children with mental or physical handicaps or personality disorders. These groups are taken in charge by the Education Services and a special programme is created for them.

Numerous groups of the blind or those with impaired vision visit the 'museum for the blind' at the Royal Museums of Art and History in Brussels. An exhibition of objects 'to be touched' is available to them in this museum. This year *Stone, from tools to works of art* enabled them to discover the use of stone in everyday objects, in architecture and in sculpture.

No museum offers a regular programme of courses devoted to teachers wishing to learn about the educational resources of the museums, though of course, study days and numerous contacts are organized whenever a meeting between the Education Service and teachers appears useful; or even indispensable, before embarking on a new programme.

It must be admitted that the museums have not the means to make satisfactory arrangements for the circulation of relevant information to the teachers. Some information is probably passed on through brochures or leaflets sent out by the Ministry of Education to all schools, but these do not appear to fall into the hands of those teachers most interested by them. The situation should be improved following the setting up of an Information Centre in Brussels this year, whose main task will be to circulate efficiently all information concerning museums and their cultural promotion programmes. Teachers receive only fragmentary and partial information about educational possibilities offered by the museums. Their collaboration in drawing up the museums' programmes is definitely on too small a scale.

In terms of documentation for schools, many museums sell cards and slides which are of particular interest to teachers and pupils. Some museums hire out slides and have one or more libraries accessible during the museum's opening hours. In many cases however, this documentation is inadequate.

A few 'portable museums' have been devised by the 'Museum-Schools' Commission of the Ministry of Education but are no longer used. A new 'portable museum' will be set up this year by the Education Department of the Royal Museums of Art and History. It will contain the history of wooden altar pieces, and show the various stages of their production; slides and photographs will evoke the social, historical and cultural context within which the exhibits were created.

The preparation of pedagogical files intended for either children or teachers is planned in various museums. This seems to us an indispensable step in order to prepare children and teachers properly for their museum visit.

The museums open their doors to diverse cultural activities: concerts, conferences, shows, films, symposia, etc. These allow the public as it were to 'discover' the museums and encourage them to come back and see the collections again. Apart from these somewhat extra-museum activities, they arrange programmes that are more directly linked to the collections: conferences and lecture visits. Within the framework of the adult education and leisure activities programme the museums offer *children's activities* in their creative workshops. The creative activity sessions organized in these workshops are centred on games and the themes suggested are in relation to the museum's collections. At the Royal Museums of Art and History in Brussels, these workshops offer programmes for *adults* too which meet with great success. The adult public participating in these workshops is different from that which takes part in the other cultural activities the museums offer. During these sessions, the adults are initiated in various techniques, the main aim being to encourage them to 'like' the works exhibited in the museum through manual creative expression. The relaxed atmosphere of the workshop greatly contributes to making this public feel at ease among the museum's contents, even though they were previously quite unfamiliar with them.

During the school holidays, certain museums offer a varied and enjoyable programme for children as well as their parents and friends.

Certain museums have considered it preferable to purchase audio-visual equipment - sound in each room or portable cassettes - so that the teacher himself can conduct an interesting visit without having to call on a member of the Education Service. Other museums install slide displays which ensure that all visitors receive a preliminary introduction to what they are to see. Finally, other museums supplement the chronological and aesthetic presentaiton of their collections by adjoining small rooms where further explanations can be given to the general public and school groups. Most Belgian museums however, do not offer visitors enough of the information to which they are entitled.

In 'Rubens Year - Museums' Year 1977', the Ministry of Education and French Culture, with the help of various museums, set up a travelling exhibition on the theme 'What is a Museum For? The Educational Resources of Museums'. Its aim is to make, in particular, teachers those in charge of Belgian cultural policy and sometimes ... the curators themselves, more aware of the educational resources of museums.

In the first part of the exhibition, methods

developed from a chosen number of works taken as examples illustrate the teaching possibilities of museur collections. The second part illustrates the means used to enable the spectator to understand and come to like the works exhibited.

During 1978-1979, this exhibition will be shown in several towns and cities in the French-speaking region of the country. On each visit, the local museum or museums will organize a special promotion programme thanks to the help of cultural promotion staff from the Fine Arts Museums and Royal Museums of Art and History in Brussels and the local authorities.

For about ten years now, the Belgian museums have really become aware of their educational and social role*, and have taken many steps on their own initiative in this field. The main task which falls upon the museums and on the Belgian political authorities today is to endow the museums with properly structured departments of education, having their own budget and personnel who are on a par with other museum personnel, thanks to having their status defined in satisfactory terms.

* The General Conferences of ICOM as well as the work of CECA have largely contributed to this awareness.

Botswana

Doreen Nteta

Botswana as an independent state has not yet achieved her first quarter century. In order to understand and appreciate the educational function of the country's museums, it will be necessary not only to consider briefly her historical and sociological situation but also the structures of her education system and of her museums.

Botswana measures 570,000 square kilometres and has a population of about 750,000. Some 85 per cent of the country is covered with Kalahari sand and the population is concentrated in the better-watered eastern areas. Surface water can be obtained on the northern and eastern part of the country; the rest of the country uses underground water supplies. As a result of this, people have three homes: those at their cultivated lands and at their cattle stations are some distance from their large home villages. In recent years, some families have moved permanently to the 'lands' or to the cattle posts, abandoning their homes in the central village. This poses problems for government in trying to provide amenities for everybody. It becomes difficult and expensive to provide for a widely dispersed population. This means that the schools in these remote areas are poor, few and badly staffed. Often large areas have no schools because not enough children can be assembled together to make the provision of a school economic. Often children have to travel miles to attend school in another village.

Botswana was a Protectorate under British rule for eighty-one years. During that period, British culture was passed on, indigenous culture became submerged, and the indigenous people began to think of their own culture as inferior to that of the ruling power and not to be encouraged. With independence came the opportunity to revive cultural heritage, an opportunity for self-assertion and for the revival of cultural identity. Institutions like the museum have helped in this regard by providing a storehouse and a visual display gallery for cultural heritage, in the form of material culture, exhibits, and oral history.

Education

In December 1975 the first National Commission on Education was appointed to review the education system which Botswana had been following since colonial days i.e. prior to 1966 when she gained independence from the United Kingdom. The commission was asked to review the education system, its goals and major problems, and to submit recommendations for improvement in education. It was evident that education had increased tremendously since 1966, if not in quality, certainly in quantity and scale - numbers of pupils, teachers and schools.

The education system has been modelled on that of developed countries and does not take into consideration factors peculiar to Botswana - population density, communications, job availability etc. The syllabus therefore has very little relevance to the country or her culture.

Among the various conclusions which emerged from the work of the commission was that the system of education had to change to accommodate changes that had taken place in society and economy. Formal education, it was found, prepared people only for white-collar jobs, and not many school leavers could find employment. There was need for a kind of intermediate school to prepare children for a life in their home villages where they can be useful.

The commission also stressed the need for non-formal, 'out-of-school', educational opportunities which can be obtained through extension services, clubs, libraries, the market place, museums and mass media.

The need for such services is made greater in rural areas because rural schools have more untrained teachers and poorer facilities. Children in the rural areas have less chance than those in urban areas of gaining access to secondary schools. Out-of-school educational opportunities proliferate because of the past lack of formal educational opportunities. About 80 per cent of the adult population is illiterate.

The commission also recommended the improvement of training opportunities, especially for teachers many of whom are unqualified.

The National Museum and Art Gallery

The National Museum and Art Gallery was established by an Act of Parliament in 1967. The necessity for a museum and art gallery had been appreciated in 1966, but at that time so many demands were being made on the Government for development funds that it was impossible to allocate any of these towards the construction of a museum and art gallery. Nevertheless, it was determined that the lack of funds should not hold up the project and an appeal was launched under the auspices of His Excellency the President. By the end of March, 1967, it was apparent that the response to the appeal would be greater that had originally been anticipated and an architect in the Government Architect's Office was appointed to draw up plans for the building. The first three galleries and an office were completed by May, 1968.

The Honorary Curator (now Director) had already commenced the collection of material. With the assistance of others, he organized and completed the first temporary display, and the museum was officially opened.

Impressed by the progress made with the construction of the building and the general organization of the museum, the Government agreed in April, 1968, to make an annual grant of R3,000* to assist with the running expenses. As a result the first member of the paid staff (the author) was appointed and sent to the National Museums of Rhodesia in May for some four months training.

By 1969 many changes had taken place in the National Museum. Apart from structural and display changes, perhaps the most important was in the attitude and understanding of the public towards the museum and its purpose in terms of development. When the idea of the museum was first mooted, many people did not appreciate that it could provide a dimension for education which it is impossible to offer in schools, particularly in the fields of cultural and natural history. Museum staff, specializing in subjects often dealt with only cursorily at schools, can provide talks and lectures on a wide range of subjects, bringing a new perspective both to students and to adults.

In 1969,the Government increased its annual grant by a further R2,000 and three town and district councils also agreed to make small annual grants towards the running expenses. During this year also two members of staff - the Assistant Curator and a trainee - received fellowships, one to study in the United Kingdom and the other in Nigeria. In 1970, three more galleries were added.

The National Museum struggled to obtain funds until, in 1973, the Danish International Development Agency (DANIDA) made a grant of R193,000 spread over a period of five years. The money was to build one more museum gallery, and auditorium and an art gallery, a storeroom and three offices. Money was also available for works of art and for recurrent costs. For most of 1973 the museum was closed to the public while permanent displays were being prepared. Work progressed very slowly and is still being carried out. Lack of really experienced staff has also militated against the rapid erection of displays of a permanent nature; nevertheless, by 1973 two fine dioramas, one of a pan scene featuring large antelope and another, a night scene of a leopard and brown hyena, both in the Kalahari, were completed.

---

* R = Rand

Of the six museum galleries at this time, one was used as a taxidermy workshop and another as an art gallery housing the work of visiting artists. So although there was no art gallery building yet, the public were not being starved of art.

For the whole of 1974 the museum remained closed to the public, but a considerable quantity of material, mainly natural history, was collected and prepared for mounting. The staff was engaged almost entirely in preparing the permanent displays. Throughout this period, school parties were allowed to go in and see the finished exhibits and the workshops. Simultaneously, the building of the extensions - the auditorium and art gallery commenced. This extension, which had been scheduled for completion by the end of 1974, was not finished until the middle of 1975 and by that time building costs had escalated and it was necessary to make cuts in the contract and to find an additional R40,000. This money was not immediately available and funds originally earmarked for buying materials, works of art, and for the construction of show cases were used to cover building costs until extra funds would be forthcoming, again from DANIDA. This hampered progress, but nevertheless more permanent displays were finished and the museum again opened to the public: the art gallery was finished and officially opened in September, 1975.

In April, 1976, the Government took over the running of the institution and since then it has been run as a Government department. As can be expected, there have been many problems, but most have been solved. This meant that the Board of Trustees had to be advisory to the responsible Minister. It also meant that the museum could not solicit and receive funds as before: estimates had to be prepared for the Ministry of Finance which already had many commitments. As a result, progress was slowed down considerably because the museum projects were not given any priority.

In spite of initial difficulties, considerable progress has been achieved. More permanent displays have been completed, the auditorium is in full use, school programmes are in operation and there are plans for an art school on museum premises and a mobile museum service aimed especially at primary schools in rural areas.

The museum teaches environmental conservation and the history of Botswana, both human and natural.

Lectures covering a variety of subjects in the human and natural sciences are held on request for schools and clubs. At the moment the staff is recording special lectures on popular topics and sending out a list of lectures, films and slide shows already available. The museum's approach is inter-disciplinary. As one walks through the galleries, one finds natural history displays next to prehistory and modern history. The visitor is drawn through a maze beginning with early man, extending through to the future development plan of the country. The exhibits are very visual and it is not necessary to read long labels in order to understand them. A *Teacher's Guide* has just been published. It explains what facilities the Museum offers and also what is available in the way of exhibits, tours and activities that the visiting group can participate in or ask to have prepared. The booklet also suggests how the teacher should prepare the pupils. Museum activities are not compulsory but since some children come once during primary school, they are encouraged to take part in some activity or other. They usually want to do anything that has been suggested to them. An experiment on activities based on Basarwa (Bushmen) artifacts proved very successful.

One problem that is encountered is that groups come to town for a day or two and during that time they want to see everything in the small capital town of Gaborone. Very often they do not realize that a visit to the museum is not like a visit to the House of Parliament. They give themselves fifteen minutes to see the National Museum and Art Gallery. Under such circumstances, little help can be given and they are left to wander. It has been found that staff can effectively handle a group of fifteen to twenty children at a time; some schools, because of distance, have to make the most of their trip and bring easily eighty to one hundred and twenty children. There is not much one can do for so many even if they had an hour to spend at the museum. This is why prior preparation by the teacher is essential. The museum has only one qualified interpreter who handles education tours. The museum also has to fit in with the group's available time for a tour because they plan their visits months ahead and transport is a problem.

Once a year, the museum sends out a letter of invitation to schools. Teachers are urged to make advance bookings, especially when bringing many children or if they want a professional guide. A visit to the museum basically means: (1) a guided tour; (2) time to answer a questionnaire prepared by their teacher or the Museum Curator of Education if she has been asked before hand to provide activities for the group; and (3) the pupils making sketches and drawings of whatever interests them - this usually results in a short illustrated essay on lions, the Kalahari, the Basarwa etc.

The museum also provides, especially for younger children, material for handling and touching and this usually results in discussion about its use or manufacture.

Often a visit to the museum is illustrated by a 10 to 15 minute slide show. Film shows are also arranged for a group of children or adults on request. The film collection is currently made up of ethnographic films.

Museum staff members give lectures to schools and clubs and societies on request. A series of lectures on biology and/or prehistory is given to university students each year. The museum has a garden of indigenous plants and some live reptiles are kept for lectures offered to students on request. Most teaching is done at the museum rather than outside because: facilities are easily available; for some students, this is their major outing for the year and they are going to be coming into town anyway to visit other places of interest; the museum has no facilities yet for taking travelling exhibitions round the schools; and the museum is short-staffed and time is best used at the place of work.

Local school children come to the museum over and over again to do projects or to continue projects started either at school or at the museum. Any follow-up work is done by the teacher at school. The museum staff always encourages the class to come back again. Special projects are encouraged and the use of the museum's reference library is offered.

1977 was a very good year for the museum and art gallery. The school programme did not really start until April, but between that time and the end of the year, museum visitors averaged between 150 and 200 per day. More visitors come during school holidays - forty-five school parties visited the museum and several classes spent whole mornings there.

In some fields, the museum has duplicates and a collection for educational purposes has been set aside.

Students are encouraged to handle material and try on clothing, etc. There is also very good archaeological material which the students may handle.

On special request, students may visit the museum storerooms and workshops. As the museum is still in the process of mounting exhibits, a visit to the taxidermy workshop is usually included even if the teacher does not ask for it. Sections of incomplete exhibits are also open to the public as it is believed the preparation of a diorama is important and educative.

The programmes which are directed mainly at primary school children do not follow the school syllabus; a deliberate attempt is made not to, unless the museum has been specifically asked by the teacher to treat a particular topic which is relevant to the school's syllabus. Children, and in fact the majority of the population, have such limited experience that it behoves every educator to try and widen their experience as much as possible.

The art gallery exhibits are African-inspired. The policy is to provide a centre of art and culture and make people aware of their cultural heritage and that of their neighbours. A collection of traditional Black art, contemporary Black art and that of other ethnic groups is being built up. The definition of art has been widened to include what might normally be considered as crafts in an effort to encourage people to take pride in their culture and to bring things to the museum. The art gallery runs temporary exhibitions of a very wide variety including works of artists from Europe, America, etc. as well as from Africa. Local artists are encouraged to exhibit and the terms for exhibiting are very generous indeed. A successful artist is asked for 10 per cent of sales whilst others may be asked to make a donation of a piece of art to the gallery.

The gallery is also involved in an Annual National Art Competition with prizes worth $ US 1,500. Most of the prizes go to children.

The museum has an auditorium in which temporary exhibitions, play readings, seminars, concerts, lectures and film and slide shows are held. Most programmes involving the museum are initiated by museum staff, unless specially requested by the visiting party.

The National Museum and Art Gallery complex is rapidly turning into a vibrant cultural centre. In association with the Botswana Society, it hosts lectures, sym-

posia and outings to places of historical or national interest in the surrounding area. It edits the journal of the Botswana Society, *Botswana Notes and Records*, and provides a link between the Society, Government and research organizations and individuals.

The museum has established a reference library, mainly for the subjects dealing with the museum and art gallery collections. There are about 2,000 books. Co-operation with museums outside Botswana has been good. Some have sent their publications regularly, and it is hoped that this will continue. The museum library has entered into an exchange system with many institutions, and very good reference material has been acquired this way.

Children's Project Room and Art Centre

The National Museum and Art Gallery has been seeking funds to build a children's centre on the museum grounds since 1976.

Although there is no building yet, the museum has already started running art courses for children who do not receive art education in their schools and for their teachers. In 1977 it obtained the free services of a trained art teacher who wanted to teach art to children and temporary accommodation offered by TEBA. The building, which is situated at the Gaborone Show Ground, is used only once a year by TEBA.

In March 1977, two art courses running concurrently were started. These ran for six months each, with thirty children from local primary schools. The courses were successful and some of the children who entered for the national art competition won prizes. Their teachers were so impressed that they asked the museum to run courses for them also. With the co-operation of the Ministry of Education, a course was started in February for thirty school teachers from the same schools as the children.

So far courses have been offered in the decorative and creative arts only, due to limitations in space and time. The programme will hopefully be expanded to include dancing (traditional and modern), music, modelling, pottery, glass blowing, printing (fabric), weaving, bee-keeping, etc. Other projected uses are lectures films and slide shows, and holiday activities in which children can pursue projects such as collecting, swopping, gardening, etc. A cafeteria, a reading corner with a small library and exhibition created mainly for children are planned.

Many children come to the museum in parties and a room is needed where they can be orientated. The centre will be used at least once a day for projects and there are already a number of volunteers who will help as and when the need arises. There are also plans to use the centre in the evenings for classes and a variety of activities.

If funds can be obtained for the centre, it is hoped that they will be enough not only for the building, but for equipment and for paying the salary of a teacher, (who would of necessity not be a national of Botswana), for paying the teacher's local counterpart (who would take over from the expatriate) and for running expenses.

It is hoped that by providing art-education for teachers, they in turn will be in a better position to guide the pupils and also help those children in their schools who will not have had the opportunity to attend any of the courses.

The National Museum and Art Gallery currently serves a population of about 200,000 people within a radius of about 80 kilometres around Gaborone. Unfortunately about 80 per cent of Botswana's population lives in rural areas, some of them very remote with no access to any intellectually stimulating and enjoyable programmes such as can be offered by institutions like the museum. It is possible to offset this lack to some degree by taking the Museum and Art Gallery to the people in the form of a mobile service. The National Museum and Art Gallery is planning to establish an extension service of its educational programme through the use of a programme consisting initially of a series of ten presentations which will cover a variety of subjects like archaeology, geology, history, art, etc. geared to the primary school educational level. The exhibits will consist of objects, photographs, slides and explanatory notes. Simple and easy to follow, they will be accompanied by an Education Officer who will explain them and show slides and films. More programmes will be developed as the need arises and interest increases.

The programme will consist of four 10-week tours in various remote, rural areas of Botswana. At certain centrally located schools, the exhibits will be set up in a class room and a presentation made to the students all through the morning session and films and slides will be shown in the evening. Each visit will last four to five days. The country will be divided into four areas to be covered over a period of two years. There will, of course, be periods when the exhibits and the vehicle will be serviced.

The schools to be visited will be selected with the help of the Ministry of Education and the District Councils, they will be notified well in advance. As the exhibits travel around, the Education Officer will make an evaluation of the project. At the end of the first phase, another evaluation with follow-up visits will be made by the Curator of Education in consultation with the Ministry of Education.

Funds for the first mobile display (three more are planned) are being provided by the United Nations Children's Fund (Unicef) through the Ministry of Education. One condition that the museum put forward was that it be given a free hand in planning the displays. The Ministry of Education accepted this and also promised to provide the first Education Officer. Plans for this for form of display are going very well. All the equipment has been ordered and some of the lectures are ready. The lectures will all be tested on the children around Gaborone first.

The author recently visited the United Kingdom to examine their education services and found that many museums have a loan service for schools. A lot of time is spent on administration,preparation of exhibits and collection and delivery of cases. On her return, various comparisons were made and both a loan service and a van that converts into a museum you can walk through were rejected; instead, the mobile display will use a small one-and-a-half ton truck with exhibits that can be taken right out and displayed in a classroom. The strong point of the exhibits is that they will illustrate lectures on specific topics. Follow-up material will be locally obtainable so that each lecture has direct relevance to the area where it is given. The problem is not in assembling the displays but in getting a good Education Officer to accompany the mobile display.

A new museum and centre has been started in Mochudi, a village 40 kilometres from Gaborone. A school built in 1921 and set on *Phuthadikobo* hill was abandoned because of drainage, transport problems, and the impossibility of expanding it as a school. This was converted into a museum with exhibits from the National Museum and from the local population; a service road was made up to the building and water was made available.

This centre will be history-oriented; it will also train artists in graphics, photography and printing. It is already being used as a centre for culturel activities and it is hoped that when developed completely, it will complement the National Museum and Art Gallery.

Conclusion

While 1977 saw much improvement in the use of facilities, 1978 also promised to be a good year. By February, there had been two school visits, one lecture outside the museum and one film loan. Members of Parliament have been talking about the museum as they visited their constituents and some have even helped with transport.

Formerly primary school leavers visited the museum; today however, children from all levels are coming. The museum is sometimes called upon to give lectures to university students on biology, Botswana history, and archaeology and public lectures by the staff are very popular. The 1978/79 budget provides for two education officers to work with the Curator of Education, and hopefully the Ministry of Education will provide a teacher to accompany the Mobile Exhibition.

The museum trains most of its personnel itself i.e. they have taxidermy trainees, one trainee cabinet-maker and one trainee in the interpretive service. Other museums help - for instance, one staff member has just returned from the Smithsonian Institution where he studied ethnology and conservation for two years.

Teacher training is the responsibility of the Ministry of Education. So far the museum has not employed any teachers because the museum , not the Ministry of Education, is responsible for its internal teaching. Because there are no teachers trained specifically for work in the musemm, and because the school's syllabus does not touch on the use of the museum as a teaching aid, the museum has had to produce a booklet to help teachers to use its facilities better.

So far the staff, under the guidance of the Curator of Education, has been able to cope. The problem is that there are no follow-up projects for most of the children who visit.

The museum is becoming more and more involved in adult education and cultural activities, especially in the arts field. It continually receives requests for courses in art and music but has been unable, so far, to do anything about them. If the art centre, which it is trying to establish materializes, then a contribution can be made towards adult education.

The museum is very well received by the public, school teachers and people connected with education. Mass media for museum programmes has not yet been used, mainly because of staff shortages. More programmes could well be held at the museum but staff and accommodation problems limit this. Even now, future galleries are being used as storerooms and workshops.

Almost all the collections have been catalogued. Volunteers are used in the library and in the preparation of lectures for schools. Some of the diorama backgrounds have been painted by volunteers.

There have been problems with the development of the National Museum and Art Gallery, but there has also been considerable progress. The idea of a museum is new to the indigenous population and its educational value is usually not understood by development planners. The museum has to compete with so many other programmes which are important in the development of a young nation, and often it is given a very low priority. It has, however, been fortunate that during its infant years the museum was a private institution. It has been hard hit by economic and political pressures which have affected the country. All the same, more and more people are realizing its worth. It has been difficult to get schools to visit the Museum with the aim of following up a project. The museum hopes to experiment with sending children out to nearby villages to see if they can collect information on various subjects such as folk tales, traditional recipes, proverbs, riddles, traditional architecture, traditional etiquette, etc.

Very often a trip is cancelled because of transport problems. The museum has no way of helping out with transport. Visiting schools come by bus, lorry or train. It is encouraging, though, to observe that visitors come from every corner of the country.

Because the museum service is young in Botswana, the Curator of Education enjoys a unique position in that she helps with the planning of displays, and is not in the periphery of museum activities. All the educational projects are based on exhibits and materials which have been specially selected with education in mind. No display is planned and finished without consultation with the museum's education department.

Canada

Maureen Gee

If there is one thing certain about museum education in Canada today, it is that the field is alive, expanding and very exciting. This became clear on reading through the hundred odd responses to a brief survey carried out by the author in 1977 concerning museum involvement in educational activities.

Education in Canada is a provincial responsibility. The ten provinces each have a department of education which administers basic funding and lays down basic guidelines and curriculum for school districts within the province. Schools in the Yukon and Northwest Territories are administered by the Territorial Councils and supported financially by the Federal Government.

Canadian museums are financed and administered in a variety of ways. There are national museums and historic sites funded by the Federal Government, provincial museums and historic sites funded by the provincial governments, and town and city museums funded by municipal governments. There are also private museums and many small museums run by volunteer societies. Funding for these may come through fund-raising activities by owners or societies; grants from municipal, provincial, or federal governments; donations of money, capital assets, services, etc., or a combination of any of these methods.

In some instances, funds for educational programmes come from the educational system. For example, in Nova Scotia the provincial museum is funded through the Department of Education. In Ontario, some regional school boards give grants to local museums which provide activity programmes for school groups. In several provinces there are instances of teachers being seconded to museums and paid for by some component of the educational system.

As might be expected, the collections held by museums in Canada range from highly specialized through eclectic to general regional, provincial and national collections. There are also a number of international collections in art, anthropology, etc. Given this diversity of collections, administration, and financing, it follows that the out-of-school activities offered by Canadian museums vary greatly.

This chapter is a summary intended to give a general description of the state of museum education in Canada today. In order to avoid terminological confusion, in the description that follows, museum education will be used to mean a planned attempt to increase communication between the exhibits and/or objects and a specific audience. Nevertheless, it must not be forgotten that in point of fact many museum exhibits are themselves didactic.

Most museum exhibits are for all age levels. However, with the exception of general tours, the vast majority of museum education programmes seems to be aimed at the grade school level (elementary ages 6 to 13, secondary ages 14 to 18). Within this age range, the level at which programmes are offered to the schools by individual museums on a regular basis seems to depend on two major determinants. The first is the collections of the museums as they relate to the school curriculum. One Quebec museum which has collections on a specific period of history offers programmes aimed at those grades during which the period of history is being taught. The second determinant is the demand for programmes. Several museums in British Columbia have found that elementary school teachers seem better able to take advantage of regularly scheduled museum programmes than teachers at the secondary levels. It is possible that this is due to scheduling difficulties at secondary schools. Consequently these museums aim most of their programmes at the elementary school level. However, determinants such as these are by no means exclusive. Most museums are willing to adapt or create programmes at the request of individual teachers prepared to work with the museum staff.

The objectives listed by respondants to the survey fall into two main types. The first are those objectives which are general to all the educational programmes offered by the museum: to increase knowledge and appreciation of national and cultural heritage; to promote awareness of other cultures; to increase skills in using museums (visual education); to enhance the educational quality of the environment (or of the arts); and to teach the value of the museum as a learning resource. The other objectives are more specific, relating to a particular programme, activity or group of activities: to improve observational skills; to promote understanding of the fur trade era; to introduce the basic geological principles; to teach the dynamics of flight; to teach the role of the fort in the early settlement of the region.

There is no doubt that these museums see themselves as both enriching and extending the education of members of the public taking part in their programmes.

Although not all museum education programmes offered are related to school curricula, the response to the survey indicates that most of those programmes aimed at grade school levels are in fact planned to tie-in as much as possible with the current curricula. Given the diversity of collections, it is obvious that the contents of the programmes cover a very wide range of topics. Some of the subject areas mentioned in the responses are history, geography, social studies, drama, art, science, geology, math, reading, and home economics.

Museums with very limited collections may offer the

same programme at a range of age levels. However, the concepts, level of information and teaching techniques are obviously adapted to suit the different age levels.

There are a number of examples of interdisciplinary programmes being offered. An art gallery with a collection of art objects which also have some historical significance will introduce the historical aspect as well as the artistic aspect of the collection. In a history museum where galleries exhibit a specific period of Canadian history, the programme may also introduce a scientific concept such as leverage, which is illustrated by the exhibit.

Programmes often show a great deal of ingenuity on the part of the museum educators. Although tours of the museum are still the major method by which museums interpret their collections, many museums, not necessarily well-staffed, are moving toward the activity (i.e. workshop) programme. Even in those museums where a shortage of space or staff make the guided tour the most logical approach, there is a move away from the traditional, explanatory tour towards a less-structured, question-and-answer method, which increases the involvement of their audiences. Many museum educators in this type of situation try to find some small corner where participants in a programme are able to try at least one 'hands on' activity.

In fact, the response in the area of activities was extremely encouraging. Many exciting programmes were reported: programmes in which children and adults are able to try out skills used by their ancestors, skills used by people in other cultures or artistic techniques which they have observed in finished works in the galleries. There are also many opportunities for participants in programmes to handle original artifacts under controlled conditions. This naturally depends on the condition of the artifact, the number of examples extant and the willingness of the curators to permit such handling, but it does indicate a move by museums across the country to increase the active involvement of their audiences with the essence of the museum - the collections.

On the subject of collections, there does not appear to be any standard policy across the country as to whether the artifacts used for handling-activities are part of the permanent collection or a part of a special education collection. Some museums reported that they used part of their permanent collections, others reported that the education division either bought, or were given by the curators, a special set of artifacts for handling activities. Still others duplicate copies of originals for handling. A number of museums also reported that 'Do touch' areas are incorporated in their exhibits to increase the involvement of casual visitors.

A wide range of facilities for educational purposes was reported by respondants. Some of the large museums reported several lecture halls, workshops, and classrooms available for activity programmes. Other museums reported only one room and still others had no space other than their actual gallery area. The numbers of persons involved on the education side of the museum work is also diverse. In a few museums there are between thirty and forty paid staff members involved in teaching programmes. Most museums report one, two or three members of staff assigned specifically for teaching duties but others report that the one-and-only director-curator is also trying to run educational programmes.

Quite a number of museums in the country are now using trained volunteer docents to teach in museum programmes. The docents are required to do extensive reading and training and are supervised by education staff members. The advantages of using volunteers are many. The training itself is an adult education activity for participants. These volunteers bring more people into the museum through their personal contacts in the community. They are, in fact, well-informed ambassadors for the museum. Volunteer docents make it possible to divide classes into small groups, thus increasing the quality of the educational experience by giving more personal attention to each student. Volunteers also make it possible for museums with small staffs to offer more programmes.

Audio-visual equipment available to museum educators varies from a complete range of movie projectors, slide projectors, video tape recorders and tape recorders to a report of one, old, temperamental movie projector.

One of the ways in which curators in museums overcome their problems of lack of space is to take their educational programmes out into the community. A number of museums report preparation lectures, slide shows or classroom visits which include the use of artifacts or specimens to prepare classes for their visit to a museum where such activities are not possible because of lack of space. There were also reports of preparation kits which might include slides, duplicates of artifacts, and background information for the teacher's use in preparing the clsss. These are often mailed out ahead of a class visit.

Large museums such as the national and provincial museums have immense geographic areas for which they are responsible. In order to provide services to their regions, they have moved into the fields of travelling exhibits and school kits. Some of the programmes involve museum educators visiting schools, which are often several hundred miles from their originating institution, and teaching with travelling museum exhibits which have been especially designed for school use. Such programmes have been extremely well received; however, they are somewhat limited due to the expense of producing such a programme.

Smaller kits of artifacts or specimens with supporting information are also circulated. These usually go by mail or freight shipment. Travelling caravans and trains also move the collections out into the community. Other museum educational activities which take place outside the museum include radio and television programmes, tours by lecturers and travelling art exhibits with animateurs.

An area of extension considered important by museum

educators is that of reaching out to classroom teachers and training them on how to use museums effectively. This field is felt to be important not only because the classroom teacher knows the students and curriculum being studied best, but also because demand for museum programmes is outstripping the museum staff capacity. Although there are programmes available at several Canadian universities for those wishing to pursue careers in museums, teachers who wish to learn how to use a museum have in the past been unable to get more than the occasional lecture during their training. One very exciting recent development is the decision by the Faculty of Education at one of the universities in British Columbia to institute a credit course (for school teachers) on how to use museums and other cultural facilities. This was offered for the first time in January of 1978.

In general, however, the museums offer programmes to teachers through open houses at the museum, and workshops held either in the museum or during teacher's conventions. University staff are making increasing use of museum educators to deliver lectures and workshops to teachers-in-training. Where teachers can be reached and trained, the process has helped reduce the load carried by museum educators, and has increased the effective use of museums by classroom teachers.

Major contact between museums is either through provincial museums' associations or through the Canadian Museums' Association. Contacts with components of the educational system varies. Some museums have contacts at the very highest levels, using the full facilities of a department of education to communicate with the school system. Others communicate through a local school board. Still others state that they feel the only fruitful contact is direct contact with the classroom teachers.

In the survey, museums were asked whether or not teachers, parents, and other outside groups were involved in planning museum education programmes. The majority replied that most of the planning is done by museum educators. However, there were reports of experienced volunteers being involved in planning programmes. There were also reports of teams of teachers planning educational activities for a museum where no education staff were available. Some museums have regular meetings with teacher groups to get suggestions for their programmes and some reported that a volunteer association in the community, with an interest in natural or human history, helps to plan the museum programmes.

The major method of publicity for museum programmes would appear to be a mailed brochure, poster, or form letter. This is sent either through a department of education or school board, directly to the school of a region or mailed to persons on a museum mailing list. However, these are not the only ways the programmes are publicized. Some of the smaller museums report that they rely on word of mouth only, and find that they have more people requesting their programme than they are able to accommodate. Larger museums may use paid advertisements on television or radio or in newspapers. All museums reported that they take advantage of any free time or space that they can get. The quality of the publicity materials which were sent along in response to the survey show that many museums have a good grasp of effective publicity techniques.

Museum educators in Canada come to the field with a wide variety of backgrounds. There are those with backgrounds in teaching and education, those trained in the various museum disciplines and those with many years of practical curatorship behind them. Few report any formal training at the university level in museum education, but most report on-the-job training. Most of them have also taken advantage of workshops and training sessions offered by the Canadian Museums' Association and by provincial museums' associations. There is a great deal of sharing either through publications or personal visits amongst Canadian museum educators. From the quality of the museum programmes being offered, it would appear that this lack of formal, institutional training is not presenting any major problems. Curators of a number of small museums who are already overworked did mention that seeing the need for education programmes made them realize a need for more training and more staff!

Museum education in Canada today is on a very exciting path, but the question being asked is, 'Where do we go from here?' There is a need for more training in the field of museum education to be made available at the university level. There is also a need for more research in this field. Despite the wide variety of programmes which are now being tried, there is still room for innovation.

Many of the problems mentioned by smaller museums are the result of poor financing. Until this problem has been overcome, many museums will have difficulty fulfilling the demands made by their public.

Responses to the survey indicate that communication between museums and components of the educational system must be improved. There are still many teachers in our school system who have not had the opportunity to learn how to use museums effectively. At present, the responsibility of training teachers on how to use museums is carried primarily by museums. It is hoped that in future, universities will carry some of this responsibility.

The idea that educational programmes are part of a museum's responsibility to its public has gained increasing acceptance in the Canadian museum community during the last ten years. Members of educational institutions are taking an increasing interest in museums as educational resources.

With the converging interest of both types of institutions, the future of museum education in Canada should be very interesting indeed.

German Democratic Republic

Manfred Kahler

The museums and the *Nationale Forschungs-und Gedenkstätten der klassischen deutschen Literatur** (hereafter referred to the *Centres*) in the German Democratic Republic make a specific contribution to stimulating man's creativity and to developing his ability to think in historical terms and to act in full consciousness of his responsibilities.

In 1953 the Government established the *Centres* with their headquarters at Weimar, the birthplace, at the end of the eighteenth and beginning of the nineteenth century, of that great and remarkable body of literature which

* National research and memorial centres for German classical literature.

entered the memory of mankind as German 'classical' literature. The thirty or so *Centres* situated in and around Weimar, like the Goethe and Schiller Archives with their important reserves and many collections, have been gathered together into one institution to which has been added the *Zentralbibliothek der deutschen Klassik** and about 150 hectares of parks and gardens. Work is currently in progress on the construction of premises for the Institute of German Classical Literature, which is taking part in the study of the *Aufklärung*** and German Classicism and Romanticism, together with the movements they inspired in other countries.

The *Centres* are both cultural and scientific. By studying this humanist heritage of abiding value as well as by maintaining it with great care and putting on public display numerous objects that bear witness to it in one form or another, those who work in these *Centres* are striving to incorporate all that is precious in their classical literary heritage with the national socialist culture.

Priority is given to methods and forms of study, maintenance and display which raise the cultural level of visitors, deepen their historical consciousness, and awaken and develop in them knowledge of the museum objects.

The work done by these *Centres* in the field of education and cultural policy forms an integral part of the State's socialist cultural policy.

By socialist culture is meant all those material conditions of life, activities, life styles and practical behaviour patterns, intellectual attainments, knowledge, ideas and ideals which are necessary for men to become the conscious creators of their history and their future, contributing, as Lenin said to the free and universal development of all the members of a society.

The permanent and temporary exhibitions and many other events and activities of different kinds put on by the museums show the importance attached to this development. Indeed, with the help of their very varied exhibitions, they contribute to the formation of a socialist view of the world and of history and make visitors capable of independent intellectual thought; encourage the systematic growth of knowledge in the fields of pedagogics, the natural sciences and

* Central Library of German Classicism
** The Enlightenment

technology, thereby responding to the demands of the scientific and technological revolution as well as to the interests and tastes of the individual; permit, in fact encourage, the introduction of the intellectual values of the past into the cultural and intellectual life of the present; and stimulate intellectual, cultural and practical creative work which in turn enriches rest, relaxation and amusement by giving them a cultural content full of meaning.

Lifelong education is an extremely important element and a matter of quasi-permanent concern to each and every citizen. This has a number of specific consequences for the education system and also for the training of adults in general. Education staff in the museums must be aware of these many and complex social relationships and contribute themselves to the solution of the problems that exist. Thus, one must constantly re-examine what the museum, as an institution, can contribute to the training and education of men throughout their lives; how, for example, can it most appropriately assist the citizen who is endowed with abilities, talents and habits he has acquired over the years? By concentrating exclusively on its educational role with school-children, the museum would not be serving its fundamental purpose.

It is already obvious that the work of the public relations directorate of the *Centres* in the fields of education and cultural policy is not aimed solely at young people, but also at groups of adults in enterprises and agricultural co-operatives. This will be clearer from the details given below.

Planned and systematic collaboration with educational authorities and establishments is based on the Socialist Education Law passed by the Chamber of the People of the German Democratic Republic on 25 February 1965. With regard to the *Centres*, this specifies in particular: assistance to kindergartens in their efforts to make use of the *Centres* for literary history as well as historical gardens and parks; help for primary school classes when they visit the museum; the part which the *Centres* should systematically play in specialized education, particularly the teaching of literature and art education; the use of museums and *Centres* for out-of-school events; and the part which the *Centres* should systematically play in teacher training and refresher courses for teachers.

As part of the curriculum in kindergartens visits are made - usually with parties of older pupils (5 to 6 years of age) - to carefully selected, small *Centres* such as the Goethe pavilion in Weimar's Ilmpark or the historical parks.

The kindergarten mistresses, or the museum's education staff, direct the children's attention to their precious cultural heritage and try to establish emotional relationships between the child, the cultural treasures of the past and nature as transformed by man. For example, museums have tried to create this particular kind of link by such simple events as looking for Easter eggs in the Goethe Garden or the Tiefurt Park.

Visits by primary school classes to *Centres* consolidate their basic knowledge of civics. Satisfying children's curiosity also develops their sense of observation. Testing them by getting them to give short talks, particularly in the higher primary classes, has contributed to the development of powers of concentration. There can be no question of this kind of museum education giving pupils of this age any more than an elementary knowledge of the life or works of Goethe or Schiller. It aims rather at creating a desire to continue visiting *Centres* and museums and to admire their precious objects.

One of the prime merits of museum education is the systematic use made in the teaching of literature of the numerous opportunities offered by the *Centres* and museums. How does this work? The curriculum of the final year in schools includes visits of perhaps one day, perhaps several days, to, say, Weimar. Under the direction of their teacher, the pupils follow a programme which consists mostly of extra-curricular activities. In general these programmes are worked out a long time in advance. The *Centres'* educational staff can thus prepare for a particular group and its specific requirements. Dates and times are arranged either verbally or, in the case of schools some distance away, in writing. When preparing a class's visit to Weimar, the *Centres's* staff concentrate on its actual content and not just on solving the organizational problems like accommodation, then the success of the whole excursion is more lasting. Teachers are advised in the preparation of the visit and provided with the appropriate material when required (museum guides, iconographic documents, slides, travelling exhibitions).

To give the teacher even more help in preparing the content of the visit and the way it is presented, as well as in the practical arrangements, there is a brochure listing the various possibilities offered by museums and *Centres* as a function of the school curriculum. Every object in the museum has not been referred to the requirements of the curriculum - only those manuscripts, books, sculptures and pictures (etchings, drawings and oil paintings) which have a connection with the subject (for example, Goethe's *Faust*, Schiller's *Wallenstein*, or Herder's *Ideen zur Philosophie der Geschichte der Menschheit*. Courses or teaching sessions are held surrounded by the original works in the museums of literature (at Weimar, for example, there are museums devoted to Wieland, Goethe, Herder and Schiller). Educational staff give advice to pupils who have particular projects to do in the museum or *Centre*. Pupils can also get information of a general nature from the information service. Frequent meetings are held with the staff of the *Centres* to discuss various set topics such as: what is the meaning of German classical literature today? what factors are decisive for understanding classicism? in what political and political-cultural conditions have the different conceptions of classicism been formed in the course of German history? Tapes and records are used in these meetings. As far as Goethe's research in the natural sciences is concerned, pupils have the opportunity of doing experiments (in, for example, the theory of colours) in a special room and with the guidance of a member of the scientific staff of the *Centres*; they can also make a detailed study of objects in the collection.

All this educational activity necessitates a continuous effort by the *Centres'* staff to analyse the literary works in question from the point of view of teaching and psychology. The planning of the sessions by different members of the staff is discussed in a group and if need be modified. When they are put into practice, further modifications are sometimes needed, particularly in regard to methods.

In his school, the teacher makes use of the knowledge he has acquired and the discoveries he has made during a visit in many different ways: first of all in his courses, in the study of works of literature, but also in the compilation of news bulletin boards in the classroom or in the school, in the designing of exhibitions in the school, or in organizing meetings with parents. From time to time there is feedback concerning this kind of fruitful spin-off. Literary dossiers,

essays, photographs and drawings are lent for information.

Help is given to schools not only in teaching but also in extra-curricular activities - for example, the meetings which the school's socialist youth organization arranges with the museum's education staff. The lectures, tutorials and discussions in most cases use the specific example of 'German classical literature' to study the problems involved in the popularization of the cultural heritage. The documents in the exhibition 'Socialism and Classicism' were used as a basis for explaining to numerous members of the Club of Young People - taking as a starting point the works of Goethe and Schiller - the various stages in the cultural revolution which followed the downfall of fascism in 1945. There are many schoolchildren who, in working groups outside school, devote themselves to the study of themes chosen from literature, the plastic arts and the theatre. They like to visit the museums and *Centres* so that they can acquire new knowledge of the work of an author who figures in their curriculum. The museum education staff do all they can to help them. Sometimes the *Zentralbibliothek der deutschen Klassik* takes part in this particular activity. The Ministry of People's Education decided in 1975, given positive and lasting experience in this regard, that all teachers preparing to teach the German language and German literature should, whenever possible, spend a week in Weimar during their studies.

Collaboration with the teacher training institutes (both colleges and universities) is another important aspect of museum education work. The aim of the student visits is to increase their knowledge of the literary movements of the *Aufklärung*, Classicism and Romanticism with the help of the documents which are on exhibit in the museums of literature. Furthermore, future teachers must be taught, as an essential part of their methodological training, to use the *Centres* and museums in their work. The advantages of practical training of this kind are obvious.

In co-operation with the Ministry of People's Education, three or four special courses are organized every year for teachers to show how German classical literature of abiding value can be used in the training of young people's socialist consciousness and in the formation of their personalities, as well as how to explain to schoolchildren the problems of maintaining cultural traditions.

The course is always based on a particular theme. In, for example, the case of a visit to Weimar for teachers of literature, the theme might be 'Problems of interpreting Goethe's *Faust*', or 'Schiller in Jena and Weimar', or 'Realism and humanism in German Classical and Romantic Literature'. There is a maximum of 120 teachers on each course, and most of the time there are more applications than places. The programme over the week includes lectures, seminars, visits guided by members of the museum's education staff, working groups, and individual work. It is not compulsory to take part in these courses. Since the *Centres* were set up in 1953, more than sixty courses have been run, involving about eight thousand teachers. Great care is taken in preparing the courses so as to give them as high an academic level as possible, for instance by securing the assistance, for the lectures, of the top literature specialists in the State.

The youth movements are part of the tradition of the German revolutionary workers' movement. Collaboration with these movements involves a series of ten events spread out over the school year helps young people of 14 years to deepen their understanding of scientific philosophy and revolutionary ethics, to act in support of socialist patriotism and proletarian internationalism and to make an active contribution to the construction of their society. In so far as they are able to, the museums help youth leaders in working out the programme of activities of the youth movements functioning throughout the State. Weimar is a city which many groups of young people want to visit, and there are two subjects with which these visits are mainly concerned:

the national memorial of Buchenwald, which teaches the young about the heroic struggle waged by anti-fascists in the concentration camp and about the strength of the working class. They draw the appropriate lessons for their own lives and current activities; and

the museums of literature and, above all, the *Centres*, which provide a setting in which to discuss in detail with the young people what is meant by 'Taking possession of everything that is true and beautiful, living the life of a cultivated man'.

The youth leaders take advantage of their visits to the museums and *Centres* to tackle the following problems with the young people in their charge, in a balanced programme worked out with the museum education staff: What is the importance of the cultural heritage for the socialist society? How do the museum treasures contribute to it? What part does culture play in the continued development of the socialist way of life? What lessons and personal experiences have literature and art already taught young people? What is the value of one's own cultural activity and the day-to-day cultural customs?

Museum education staff are available to answer questions. An outing by young people naturally requires, like any visit to a museum, intensive planning and preparation. Special courses are held in co-operation with the appropriate institutions of the district or region; the youth leaders familiarize themselves with a youth outing as it might actually be conducted in the Schiller House or the Goethe House at Frauenplan.

The way of life in the German Democratic Republic, which is based on the socialist mode of production, is centred on continuously raising the material and intellectual standard of living. Concscientious, honest work which is useful to society is one aspect of this; another is a high level of culture and development of the interests and needs of the workers in the intellectual and cultural fields. This is one of the decisive reasons for the rapid increase in visits to museums and exhibitions by the workers in the State.

In accordance with the idea of culture as comprising and bringing together intellectual and material values, the working class regards as its heritage not merely the arts but also the values acquired in production and the transformation of nature and through study of the sciences as well as of practices and customs.

The engineers, foremen and group leaders all quite rightly expect advice from the museums in preparing these trips, excursions and cultural events. The greatest attention is given to providing this advice. However, the ideas and requests of the enterprises sometimes go beyond the possible, in which case judicious adjustment is necessary.

Workers are often prepared for their visit to Weimar in a practical way, with talks illustrated by slides. Travelling exhibitions put on in enterprise clubs or restaurants also help to make them aware of the *Centres* or of the work of a particular author. As far as possible given the available staff, the workers' own occupational training is used to familiarize them with the role of the cultural heritage in the socialist society. Training is also given to those in charge of cultural clubs, centres, etc., in collaboration with their trade union organizations.

The Goethe *Centre* at Kochberg Castle, the former seat of the von Stein family, underwent a long and complicated restoration before eventually being opened to the public in 1975. Courses were then held there, to enable club organizers and other cultural leaders from the Erfurt region to gain a thorough knowledge of the *Centre*. In the months that followed, these people themselves brought groups of workers along to the castle for extended visits. The entire site - the *Centre*, the museum and the lovely historic park - is ideally designed to satisfy the requirements of culture, rest and relaxation.

The internal newspapers of the big factories in the Erfurt region also carry articles by the staff of the *Centres* about new exhibitions, various art objects, etc.

There are written agreements with a number of enterprises which contain specific examples of the way in which the *Centres* contribute to the development of the personality and enable the workers to enjoy cultural experiences that enrich their lives.

The *Centres* organize other series of regular events which are becoming increasingly popular both with local people and with visitors. The press - and sometimes the regional radio programmes - gives the monthly programme of what is on in the city. Particular attention is given to the discussions every other Sunday on various works, manuscripts or iconographic documents in the *Centres* and museums and to the festivities organized to commemorate the birthdays of Goethe or Schiller.

Every Easter, events are organized in the museums and *Centres* in conjunction with the city's cultural and scientific authorities. The 'Youth Days of Weimar' have been held every July since 1959, with apprentices, young workers, pupils and students taking part in extremely lively discussions on the cultural heritage. For several years now, young workers of Weimar have been giving very useful assistance to the education staff of the *Centres* in welcoming numbers of young visitors to the *Centres*.

The numerous visitors to the *Centres* and museums - and there were more than a million of them last year - mean that more technical methods have to be used for such things as brief introductions. The texts of these introductions and the talks which are tape-recorded and accompanied by slides require particular care. Their impact depends not only on what is selected from the many documents available but also on the way in which the material is presented, from the point of view of educational psychology.

A good example is the success achieved by the sound track used for visits by school groups to the Goethe *Centre* at Stützerbach, a place which is both a summer resort and somewhere to take a cure. Leaflets, brochures and notices are all good preparatory material for a visit to the museum; they help the visitor to find his way about and to think about what he has seen and heard.

The specialized working groups of the *Centres* attach great importance to the conscientious preparation of this kind of material, with all due regard to educational considerations.

The fact that visitors tend to throng to such major international *Centres* as the Goethe House at Frauenplan or the Schiller House at Weimar will necessitate in future marshalling people to a greater extent so as to avoid as far as possible the congestion created by school groups and tourists arriving at the same time and thereby to ensure that the many German and foreign visitors enjoy better conditions for their visits and studies. Work has already begun along these lines.

Iran

Marie Shaibaie

Iran is a country going through a period of tremendous progress and expansion, and this is reflected in the pressures of museum educational facilities. Museum educational activities currently are directed towards establishing a sense of national identity through the development of recognition of and pride in the country's national heritage. A second objective is the stimulation of creativity.

The Department of Museums initates all educational activities involving museums. Their programmes are directed primarily towards eighth graders, that is, the 12 to 14 age group, and relate to social science courses in particular, although there is some involvement with other subjects. Within the museums themselves, guided tours are arranged and lectures are given occasionally, the latter involving the students in writing follow-up essays. Other programmes include national contests and comparisons of paintings, involving the writing of short essays.

However, the most important programme does not take place within the museums themselves. This is the Mobile Museum * programme which consists of taking the museum to the students in the form of slides, films, tapes, lectures and artifacts.

The Mobile Museum travels the country with a team of six, moving from town to town and city to city, setting up its exhibits wherever possible. A typical setting would be an auditorium, long and narrow, with seating for fewer than 500, its walls decorated with posters and black and white photographs of artifacts from different eras and regions of Iran. Some forty artifacts would be exposed on shelves.

The arrival and opening of the Mobile Museum is usually marked by a lengthy ceremony involving local dignitaries and including the presentation of the complete programme. The programme, aimed as it is at school-children, is fairly simple. A short colour film is presented, showing how early man may have created pottery and indicating those forces which inspired him to paint his pots with primitive geometric and naturalistic designs. It goes on to trace the methods used in excavating artifacts and the steps which eventually lead to their display in a museum.

The film is followed by a slide presentation of examples of artifacts and architectureal monuments spanning Iranian history. The final part of the programme involves the children wandering through the display of artifacts, preferably in small groups.

The two inspectors who reported on the Mobile Museum described it as an essential project, filling a great need in the country by acquainting pupils in areas where there are no museums with their rich cultural heritage and identity. They also made the following ten recommendations.

* The information concerning the Mobile Museum is taken from a report written by two inspectors, Faranak Ghaffari Van Patten and Phyllis Renee Macklin.

1. The short film is good, but due to different climatic conditions and constant showings, the condition of the film has deteriorated. There should be more than one copy available for showing.

2. There should be colored, well mounted photographs with typed complete captions. The photographs of artifacts should represent a broader historical picture of Iran. The present photographs are in very poor conditions.

3. The brochures should be sent to the schools before the visit of the Mobile Museum, along with a description and photographic sampling of the artifacts and other pertinent information so that the students are well informed prior to the programme.

4. A large map of Iran showing the locations where the artifacts were found would be instructional.

5. The students should be broken up into groups of ten and led through the exhibit with one guide.

6. The responsible teachers or principal and one team member should help in the general supervision and traffic flow during the viewing of artifacts.

7. A chronological table with the appropriate dates, dynasties, and other pertinent facts relating to the artifacts should be given to the students.

8. A camera would be useful for the team to record the activities of the Mobile Museum and the reactions of the children.

9. There should be a complete yearly evaluation of the programme and work should continue on the Museum even when it is not on the road. This would provide for an orderly continuity.

10. Each year, the Mobile Museum should have a theme which could be projected through the film, the speeches and the artifacts, thus enabling regular return visits to the same areas.

The Department of Museums is experimenting with new ways and means of reaching students and the population in general. Plans for the future involve the establishment of regional museums in different provinces to bridge the gap between yesterday, today and tomorrow. Activities that are impossible in crowded schools will then have an opportunity to bloom and museums will be able to fulfill their goal of contributing to developing well-balanced and culturally-aware men and women whose abilities will create a better land for the people to come.

Mali

Oumar A. Konaré

The National Museum of Bamako's programmes are intended for all age groups, even though certain programmes are designed particularly for young children under 8 years of age. For a long time, most exhibitions were permanent. However, due to lack of space, there is now a new policy of organizing temporary exhibitions so as to vary the themes. This policy also facilitates the conservation of additions to the collection. These often multidisciplinary programmes deal mainly with art and history. Nevertheless, there are some specifically educational activities, including guided visits of the exhibition galleries and even the storerooms. More and more activities outside the museum are being developed, such as travelling exhibitions and conferences given in schools themselves by museum staff.

The participation of schools in preparing exhibitions is at present limited to the production of advertising posters and explanatory texts. Certain schools themselves organize exhibitions based on pupils' work: exhibitions of paintings by the National Art Institute, or exhibitions of the results of practical work by the Vocational Training Centre, teacher-training centres and the Young Pioneers. School participation, is frequently encouraged, sometimes by the press, sometimes by written invitations.

Among museum visitors, there is a high percentage of pupils and schoolteachers. The only group visits recorded are those from schools. Many pupils, however, visit the museum alone. These visits are rarely prepared for in advance. There are no brochures or catalogues on the exhibitions, nor are there special collections devoted solely to educational activities. The collections were not conceived in relation to educational curricula.

After each visit to an exhibition, the pupils' opinions are collected verbally and then registered in the visitors' book. The opinions of schools which have visited the National Museum present certain characteristics, as can be seen from the examples below: a feeling of gratitude for having discovered one's culture and one's past; regret for the lamentable state of the National Museum; and a wish for an improvement in working conditions.

'We, the 4th Year A students, are pleased to visit this museum - it is so rich in souvenirs and shows how great our country is.' (Pupils from Medina-Coura A School)

'The girls from N'Tominkorobougou B School are satisfied with their visit to this museum. We hope to find a large gallery in the future.' (N'Tominkorobougou B School)

'My pupils and I have greatly benefited from this visit and we have spent a pleasant time with the museum guides whose clear and precise explanations were appreciated.' (Brehima Samaké, science teacher)

'A very interesting and instructive visit.' (The children from the Czechoslovak Embassy)

'I found out more about myself in discovering these treasures, which contain a wealth of my past. I can only be proud to have in my possesion such riches which do honour to my country.' (B.S. Doumbia, student at the National School for Administration).

However, the school is not the only educational institution in our country. In addition, its origins are foreign and it has not yet been integrated into the traditional structures of education. The family and other traditional institutions of education (esoteric and cultural associations and peer-group associations) ignore the existence of the museum and have no contact with it. For them, the museum, like the school, damages the child and destroys the country's values. One result of this is that the museum's educational activities remain very modest, due to the very conception of the museum itself, the problems facing schools in Mali and the museum's material problems.

The museum, seen as a centralized institution responsible for safeguarding the cultural heritage, is not an authentically African institution. Rather, the objects and artifacts making up the country's heritage remain in the ancestral treasure house or the sacred wood in each village. With no national funds at its disposal the museum has been unable up to now to acquire any of this wealth of artifacts belonging to Mali's cultural heritage. It has been ignored, just as schools were at the offset.

During colonization, the museum worked with foreign concepts and presented African culture only as an art-form and as folklore. It appealed essentially to foreigners or tourists or a national élite, often severed from its natural roots.

The museum's austere nature was offputting. Moreover, its programme essentially looked back to the past and it was basically concerned with conservation. This conception of the museum could only lead to a conservative, wait-and-see attitude, a pruning-back of museum activities, a lack of initiative and a failure to make contact with other educational institutions such as schools.

On the side of the schools too there are obstacles hindering contacts with the museum. Even if the school structure covers the whole of the country, it is not sufficient to eliminate illiteracy. Sixty per cent of Malians are under 20, and many children do not go to school; there are nearly 250,000 children in school for 1,500,000 applicants, corresponding to an enrolment rate of just under 15 per cent.

Not only are there not enough permanent premises; there is also a shortage of teachers - not all classes in the country have a teacher, and many classes have enormous numbers of pupils. Some first year classes (6 to 8 year olds) have nearly ninety pupils; ninth year classes (15 to 17 year olds) have nearly fifty pupils; twelfth year classes (18 to 20 year olds) have nearly thirty five pupils. School curricula are overloaded and somewhat rigid. The adaptation of curricula to contemporary national needs is far from completed. The number of class-hours is very high and nearly all classes are held indoors. Open-air classes, which inspire increased awareness of the surroundings, are only used as occasional back-up. Added to this, the working-hours in schools coincide with the museum's opening hours.

Within the museum itself, the efficient functioning of educational activities encounters numerous difficulties, in terms of the collection, personnel, premises and financing.

The *collections* include artifacts, essentially of two types, archaeological and ethnographical. The majority are of the former type, harpoons, grinders and pottery sometimes intact, sometimes fragments. The ethnographical artifacts include masks, statuettes, musical instruments, vases and household objects such as stools and tobacco boxes. Although these objects are representative of the main ethnic groups in Mali (*Bamanan, Malinké, Senufo, Dogon)*, many other ethnic groups are not yet represented. Artifacts tend to be poorly conserved, which makes handling difficult, and there are not enough to mount large exhibitions. Added to this, their documentation remains incomplete as numerous among them are as yet unidentified.

The *staff*, which numbers roughly a dozen, is insufficient. Mainly composed of teachers or museum technicians, it is completely preoccuppied by the internal workings of the museum, (i.e. inventory, conservation, preparation of exhibitions, etc.). In addition, there are no highly specialized staff everyone excercises the function of curator, technician, archivist, educators, etc. simultaneously.

The National Museum does not have its own *premises*. Rather, it is dispersed throughout the town - store rooms in one place and exhibition gallery and offices in another, thereby making access difficult, particular-

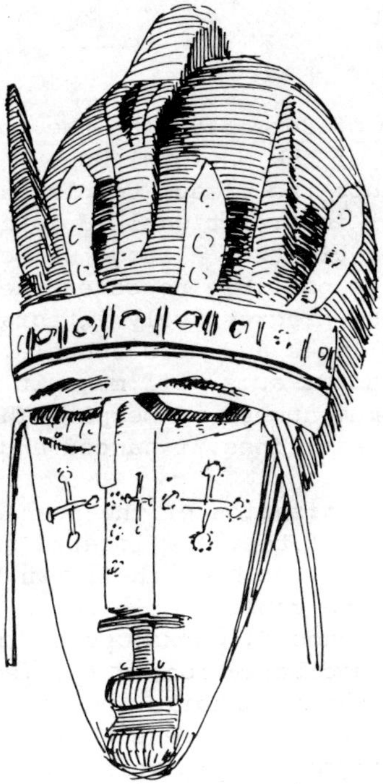

ly as schools have not means of transport. The museum premises are singularly small and lack both special arrangements for ventilation, lighting or air-conditioning and special rooms for educational activities (cinema or lecture room), laboratories, and recreation courtyards. The equipment, in particular the audio-visual material, is quite insufficient.

The National Museum suffers *financial difficulties* and is always short of funds. While education is allocated 30 per cent of the National Budget the former receives an indirect budgetary allocation, and under present circumstances has little prospect of raising enough revenue to meet its own expenses. The National Museum has no source of aid (Friends of the Museum, benefactors' associations, etc.), apart from the State.

These are the problems facing museums in most under-developed countries. However, the present evolution of the conception of museums and museum policies paves the way for an improvement of the situation. By decentralizing and democratizing the museums, it becomes possible to assign them a place among the government's priorities in the country's overall development. This new policy which has been adopted in Mali has several facets.

First, in term of democratizing the conception of museums, the fact of the National Museum existence does not in itself enable the museum to play an important role in schools or in traditional educational institutions. However, by creating a large number of local museums, it will be possible to cover the whole of the country and thereby progressively integrate museums into the peoples' lives and into schools. The establishment of specialized museums will make it possible to interest the maximum number of people. These museums will be run on modest lines, financed and maintained by local authorities.

Secondly, democratization of the means of access to museums is possible if they are located carefully to cater to those who do not have their own transport. The museum should also be mobile, able to go out into the streets, squares, schools, workshops and places of work.

Thirdly, the democratization of the means of communication within the museum entails the use of national languages, thereby enabling pre-school children and those just starting school, as well as those who have been unable to obtain a place at a school, to join in more effectively.

Fourthly, democratizing programmes implies a content reflecting the population's aspirations and enhancing the old traditions which are disappearing. The museum's programmes can support those of the schools and, furthermore, they can undertake post-school teaching, thereby becoming centres of traditional education.

Fifthly, democratizing responsibilities reflects acceptance of the fact that the participation of representatives of community organizations, traditionalists and teachers in the supervision and elaboration of the museum's action programmes is indispensable.

Teachers and students alike should follow what is going on in the museums, through the intermediary of associations (Friends of the Museum) or of commissions for safeguarding the cultural heritage.

Parallel to the measures suggested above, others now in practice should enable the museum to fulfill its conservation, research and cultural promotion role.

These measures include plans for building, in the very near future, a National Museum functional because it complies with modern museological norms yet not offputting by its structure or appearance, blending well with its environment. It will provide extensive facilities for laboratory work and conservation, while the local museums now under consideration will be primarily concerned with collection and cultural promotion. The present National Museum is itself already in the process of being renovated. The permanent exhibition gallery has been transformed into storage space in order to facilitate the inventory and the conservation of all objects. The Museum will organize temporary thematic exhibitions in Bamako and travelling exhibitions throughout the country.

Another measure involves stressing the collection and restoration of objects. In addition to the traditional means of acquiring objects (donations, purchases, exchanges and requisitions), bi-annual cultural and artistic displays by young people and school children will be used as an opportunity for acquiring new objects. Furthermore, the National Museum is hoping to obtain financial autonomy, which will allow their activities to bring it in some revenue.

Several measures are under consideration in terms of organizing work: the museum staff members will be specialized and each will have a clearly defined task. Thus it will eventually be possible to create an 'education' department capable of taking the initiative in several spheres (e.g. organizing games and competitions) and of suggesting reforms to the school curricula, for example, that the teaching of drawing and music be a real aesthetic and artistic education and that the curricula be more 'Malianized'. The department's reflections will take into account traditional forms of society, mainly the family. Its aim will be to make it possible for traditional societies to express themselves, give vent to their cultural traditions and at the same time come to terms with the phenomena of modern life.

The school and the museum, both foreign institutions, must learn to embrace with Malian society. Only 'another school', only 'another museum' can so embrace the Malian context. The teaching reform under way since 1962 and the new museum policy adopted in 1976 pave the way for this change. These two institutions should aim at forming Malians living in peace with environment and participating in its harmonious transformation.

Mexico

Rodolfo Peltier

In Mexico, there are several institutions under the Government responsible for establishing museums. The Ministry of Eudcation, through the National Institute of Anthropology and the National Institute of Fine Arts, is the main government organization creating museums all over the country. Other public institutions and regional governments also undertake the task, but mainly in collaboration with the institutions mentioned above. Private museums are few; they are not dealt with here, because they do not have educational programmes. Usually they are used for lectures and film shows not related with the collections of the museum.

The National Institute of Anthropology and History

has created an organized museum system: national, regional, local and school museums, covering the whole country. The National Institute of Fine Arts has several museums, mainly in Mexico City and in the countryside, museums associated with cultural centres. The Federal Commission of Electricity has built the Museum of Technology, the only one of its kind in Mexico. The Department of Federal District (the Mexico City Government) has two important museums: the Museum of Mexico City and the Museum of Natural History.

Mexico City has the largest number of important museums, in size, quality and organization. But in spite of this, these are not enough to satisfy the needs of around twelve million inhabitants in the metropolitan area. The situation is no better in the rest of the country, with more than fifty million population and proportionally fewer museums to cover their necessities. Generally speaking, most of the museums outside Mexico City do not have formal educational programmes, apart from a few regional museums. Some local museums have educational facilities, organized by the local school children. One of the aims of local museums is to provide people from the community with educational experience in the building and organization of the local museum.

In this survey of educational programmes in Mexican museums, only the museums with the most intensive educative activities are considered. They are found mainly in Mexico City and in some regions of the country. The sample shows the general trend of educational programmes; perhaps some fine examples of museums are lost but is was impossible to cover all the existing museums and probably it will not affect the results of this work.

The educational system in Mexico is both public and private. Public education is predominant and it is under the Ministry of Education. There is an educational reform and a national plan of education is in preparation. Both contemplate the use of museums as a part of the educational school programmes.

Programmes Offered

The educational programmes in Mexican museums are aimed first of all, at primary school children, aged six to twelve years (they are the majority of visitors belonging to the school system - 250,000 children per year at the NMA*); next, at secondary and preparatory students, aged thirteen to eighteen years, and teachers; and finally, at adults in organized groups and the general public.

The educational system in Mexico includes in its school programmes compulsory visits for students, elementary and secondary levels, to museums, thereby utilizing the museum as a pedagogical aid and taking advantage of the educative activities offered. However, due to a lack of transportation, and sometimes of interest on the part of school teachers, these visits are sometimes dropped from the programme.

Elementary and Secondary General Directorates schedule visits to museums in co-ordination with the educational departments of each museum, according only to arranged days and hours. Teachers choose which museums to be visited and when, depending on their school programmes and curricula. This is up to the teachers because museums do not cover school subjects specifically.

Nevertheless, a great number of members of the educational staff and guides of museums are former teachers, from the elementary and secondary levels (and hired because of this), who know the educational programmes and school subjects well and can therefore relate the visit to the school visitors interest.

Contents and Methods of Museum Education Activities

The goals of the museum's educational activities are to help visitors to a better understanding of the works of mankind, interpret the meanings of the collections in a pedagogical way and to organize different activities to stimulate the imagination and understanding of the audiences.

---

* Abbreviations of the museums studied: National Museum of Anthropology (NMA); National Museum of Cultures (NMC); Museum of Modern Art (MMA); Museum of San Carlos (Art Museum) (MSC); Museum of Technology (MOT); Museum of Natural History (MNH); National Museum of History (NMH); Museum of the City of Mexico (MCM); Museum of Art Carrillo Gil (MAC); Regional Museum of Guadalajara (RMG); and Regional Museum of Puebla (RMP).

The museum's educational services, according to the survey, primarily involve guided tours to museum's collections for children, beginning with an introductory lecture - films or slide shows - a visit to one or two rooms and visit to an educational exhibit, when there is one (orientation room, NMA, or the historical fact of the month, NMH), finishing with a workshop where the children make drawings, model plasticine or write essays from their museum experience. This kind of visit is made in a single day and takes from two to four hours. The group's size is on average thirty to forty students.

National museums have special afternoon and evening programmes for preparatory students (age fifteen to eighteen years) held in three meetings, and programmes for adolescents and adults in eight or ten meetings. Both programmes consist of lectures, films and guided tours to collections. Helped by the educational staff, curators are in charge of these programmes. Other museums have workshops of artistic expression, with classes for painting, drawing and collage (MSC) or technical shows for students of all ages (MOT).

Several museums have a one-month vacational programme for children and youngsters, with workshops in painting, art crafts, drama, puppets, etc., related to the museum's subjects and collections, with the collaboration of curators and other specialized staff (NMC, NMH, MCM). Museums also offer special guided tours and lectures to groups of factory workers, government and private employees, etc., during the day and at convenient hours. The Museum of Natural History is the only one which combines activities in the museum with excursions to collect and classify specimens during vacational programmes.

The majority of museums have audio-visual material: films, slides and tapes for the use of educational activities, lectures, panels and meetings aimed at the general public. Concerts, dramas, films, dances and lectures contribute to the daily activities of museums.

Many museums in Mexico do not have adequate facilities for educational purposes. Good examples of colonial buildings were adapted to be museums, which makes it impossible to change or make the right installations for educational and related activities. But almost all the museums have small or medium-size auditoriums which are used as classrooms or workshops. They rarely have educational activities outside the museum building itself. Occasionally, educational staff give lectures or slide shows in schools or other institutions. The only museum which has outside activities is the National Museum of Anthropology. There are no loan collections or kits at all. There are some travelling exhibitions, but they are destined for other museums in the country. There is not a single museum with special collections for handling. Only the museum of Technology has exhibits with knobs and cranks which the visitors can manipulate. The National Museum of Anthropology has a special programme for the blind, but they use the same objects which are displayed in the permanent exhibitions.

Two museums have exhibitions adapted for educational programmes: the Orientation Room (NMA) has a display of small replicas of archaeological monuments, with mobile pieces and taped music and lecture, operated by computer. The historical fact of the month (NMH), a temporary monthly exhibit, has original pieces of the museum's collection and an interpretation which relates the historical moment to the present situation. Several museums mount exhibitions showing the results of the workshops at the end of the year (NMA, NMC, MSC, etc.).

Some museums are experimenting with educational activities carried out by individuals or organized groups, without the presence of the educational staff, i.e. printed guides, which mark out the rooms and collections, and have empty spaces to be filled in by writing or drawing the necessary information contained in the very same exhibitions (NMC).

Organization of Museums' Education Activities

Organization is carried out by the educational staff of museums, sometimes with the help of the specialized personnel. School authorities, teachers and pupils do not participate. The role of school authorities is to co-ordinate the visits of the school groups to museums.

Many museums in Mexico have activities in co-operation with private companies (industries, etc.) to organize visits of technological students to factories and working centres; lately, museums have been included to cover the cultural aspect of this training.

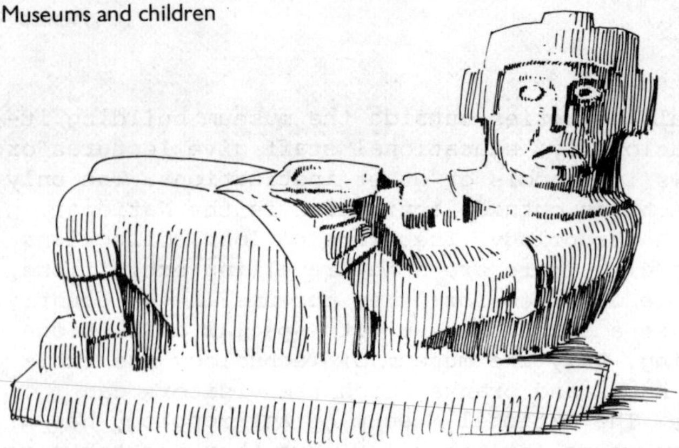

The Roles of Museum Staff and School Teachers in Educational Activities in Museums

School teachers have no role in planning museums' educational activities. On some occasions they prepare their school group's visit beforehand with the museum staff. Sometimes school teachers have to conduct their school group's visit themselves, because there is not enough museum staff, the visit is out of schedule or the specific topic they want to teach using the collections is too specialized (MOT, MNH). But there is no permanent contact or link between the museum and local schools, and no consultant or planning group exists.

Several museums have teacher training, aiming to show teachers the best way to use the educational resources of museums, to acquaint them with the collections, to help them interpret and transmit more useful information to their pupils, and to give them a more specialized knowledge about related subject matters of interest in their professional careers.

Educational museum staff is trained in the museum by members of the educational department and specialized personnel through lectures, guided tours of collections and short course with the curators.

Information

Each institution has its own system for giving information about education activities in their museums: the National Institute of Anthropology and History publishes a monthly brochure with all the cultural and educational activities in their museums while the National Institute of Fine Arts has a similar system using posters and leaflets. Other museums do not have this kind of information, but every museum reports its activities, schedules and programmes to the school authorities. Many museums use the press to advertise their activities. There is no publication collecting every possible programme for all the museums.

Schools - mainly private - and other institutions are approached regularly by telephone calls and letters. Several museums do not do this - the demands for educational services are overwhelming and there is not enough staff to attend them. Some museums personally contact working centres and adult groups to organize education activities for them.

Problems and Future Plans

The main problem faced by educational museum's programmes is financial. The greater part of budgets is for maintenance, collections and personnel salaries. There is a scarcity of professional staff specialized in education, both in term of number and qualifications. The survey shows from two to eighteen members in the educational departments.

Space is another problem: in many museums, it is difficult to solve because of the types of buildings used as museums. This problem also accounts for a deficiency of facilities to handicapped visitors.

Many museum educators complain about a lack of interest on the part of school teachers, probably because there is no collaboration between schools and museums in organizing efficient and dynamic education programmes. There is even a lack of co-ordination between museums belonging to the same institution.

The general impression is that Mexican museums are not using educational resources to their full potential as educational instruments. This is reflected in the educational methods of several museums, where there is no taking into account of any innovation or imaginative system to develop more interesting educational programmes.

A few museums reported future plans, including the adaptation of free spaces in the museum building for workshops, classrooms, children's rooms, etc. and more adequate teacher training and special programmes for adults from the less educated levels.

University Museum of Arts and Sciences (University of Mexico) The Museum is located on the university campus. There is no permanent exhibition, just temporary ones lasting several months. The topics of the exhibitions are numerous, embracing a variety of themes concerning art, anthropology, sciences, design, costumes, etc. Simultaneously many activities are carried out, closely related to the exhibtion: films, lectures, panels, music, drama, dance, etc., aimed at exhausting all possible knowledge to be gained from the exhibit. The museum periodically offers a workshop for children on Saturday mornings, conducted by the educational museum staff with the help of different specialists. The purpose is to make participants sensitive to the idea of creativity, through interdisciplinary subject matters: from literature, dance, plastic arts, pantomime, music and songs to theatre. The workshop has a duration of around two months, and is not necessarily connected with the museum exhibits.

Gallery of History (National Institute of Anthropology and History) This gallery is situated next door to the National Museum of History and it is an educational instrument by itself. Exhibits are a display of dioramas with replicas from the National Museum of History collections. Along with the exhibition there are slides and films, and works and music on tape.

The gallery has been designed in accordance with the public school system programmes and text books. It covers Mexican history from the end of the Spanish colony to the 1910 Revolution. Five guides (teachers) conduct tours for school children groups and adults. Some visits are complemented with painting lessons.

Casa del Museo - Museum House (National Institute of Anthropology and History) The 'Casa del Museo' is a branch of the National Museum of Anthropology and has its own staff. It is a neighbourhood museum located in a slum area of Mexico City. Its aims are to educate the residents of this poor area, to contribute to the betterment of standards of living through permanent and temporary exhibits showing how the history and culture of the country relates to their own situation, and to help them understand their problems and find solutions.

Exhibits and activities are worked out with the help of the people from the area, especially children and teenagers. Temporary exhibits are designed to describe actual facts of the place, cultural habits, food and housing, etc., and how they can be changed for the better.

The staff is a mixture of professionals who are together to create a new experience on the role of museums. They are specially prepared to stimulate the imagination of children and to answer any questions. There is a direct communication between the staff and the audience; they put together most of the activities of the 'Casa del Museo'; programmes are animated by films, popular music, Latin American folklore, games and sports.

The museum's programmes are not rigid, but changing and constantly corrected by taking into account criticisms and suggestions; they are permanently experimenting.

School Museums (National Institute of Anthropology and History) This programme works in elementary and secondary school levels and has two main purposes: to motivate students, teachers and members of the communities, through the school museum, to respect and to learn about the country's cultural and natural patrimony; and to use the collections as a basis for study and to make the school museum an integral part of the school using it as a pedagogical aid.

The school museum idea is encouraged by the programme's cultural promotion officers (teachers with special training) because the participation of schools has to be accepted by the educational authorities, school teachers and students. If the response is positive, the promoter organizes a committee in each school with five students, two teachers and two parents, all elected by all the school members. The committee is the representative of the school community and is in charge of the necessary work to create the museum and to organize all the activities around it. The cultural promotion officer periodically gives advice and guidance in the classification of collections, museography, etc. The museum is installed in areas not used in the school building, such as an empty class room, corridors, or even storerooms. Students ask the community for materials, ranging from wood to make the showcases to objects to be exhibited in the museum. They also collect samples of minerals, plants, animals and archaeological and ethnographical materials, paintings or old photographs, and everything they would like to have in their museum. They contact people from their community to learn about local history, traditions, habits, community economy, etc., to represent this information in the museum. They trade with other schools museums to obtain objects and information from different parts of the country.

Collections are divided into natural and social sciences or, in a broader sence into Man, his culture and environment.

There are now around 700 schools under the programme, 70 per cent in rural areas and the rest in urban areas, covering seven States of Mexico and Mexico City as well. The sixty cultural promotion officers doing field work receive specialized support in anthropology, history, museography, etc. from a small staff in Mexico City.

Nigeria

Emmanuel Nnakenyi Arinze

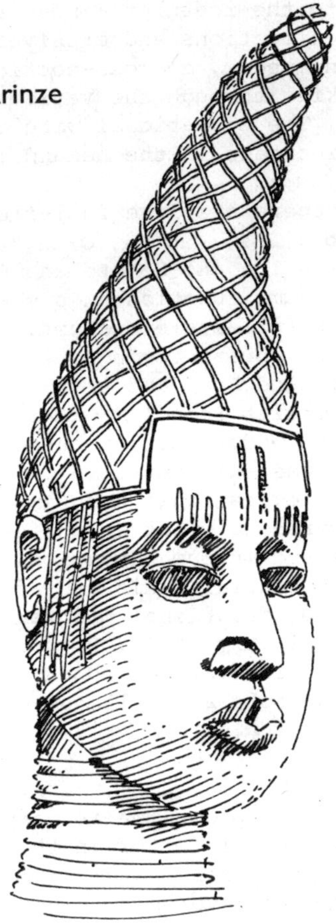

In Nigeria, the museum as an institution is becoming an important factor in socio-cultural and educational activities. More and more people now use museum facilities in various ways. There has been a tremendous increase in museum visitors covering the entire spectrum of the Nigerian public, ranging from pre-school children to university students, and including adults who just come to the museum on their own to gain knowledge and enjoyment. Visitors also include the 'illiterate' who, although they cannot read or write English in the Western sense, still find satisfaction in coming to the museum. To this group, the objects on display tell a story. In addition, museums cater to the research-minded academic who spends time perusing collections and archives. Thus one finds, in any Nigerian museum, a cross-section of the public mixing and walking through the various galleries in a relaxed manner. The educational wing of the museum is faced with an increase in the demand for educational activities.

At present, there are five full-fledged national museums in Lagos, Jos, Kaduna, Oron, and Benin City. In other cities like Ibadan, Sokoto and Port Har-Court, the national museums function on a smaller scale as they are not yet full-scale museums. In addition, there are local museums spread throughout the country in Owo, Ife, Esie, Kano, and Aba, and a small school museum in the Government Crafts School Pankshin near Jos. University museums come under another authority. The first national museum was only built in 1952 in Jos, while the first formal educational programme was started in 1969. Thus compared to other countries with a long history of museums and museum education, Nigeria is still developing her potential. This has affected the development of museum educational programmes as the unit concerned is still very young. However, efforts are being made to provide various educational services, especially for schools and colleges.

Objectives

The museum education programme is based on the belief that culture is a vital factor in the development of any nation, its personality and its national identity. This is very true in developing countries that have passed through colonialism which left its mark on the cultural and national life of the people. Museum educationalists therefore aim at building up the history of Nigeria by putting together the various cultural materials and records that have survived through the ages, from the stone age through Nok, Igbo-Ukwu, Ife, Owo and Benin to the modern times. By doing this, they hope to set records right and place their history in the right perspective.

Programme

Museum education activities are organized to cater for various age-groups: children (7 - 12 years); students

(12 - 21 years); youth (18 - 24 years); and adults (25 and above). There are different programmes for each age group, although in some cases the programmes are merged. For instance, the National Museum in Lagos shows films and organizes live cultural performances and dances monthly as part of its adult education programme.

Over the years, this museum has been able to collaborate with schools in teaching certain subjects, i.e. Social studies, History, Art, and Art History and African Studies. To achieve this, extra mural museum activities have been developed which include: giving lectures in schools on topics that are based on the school syllabus but best taught with museum aid, using museum objects as visual aids in the class-room during lessons; and sending museum personnel to schools to help teachers develop lessons that are best taught with museum materials.

As a follow-up, a lecture series with slides is being developed on various topics like Benin Art, Ife Art, Nok Art, Igbo-Ukwu Art, Owo Art and 2000 Years of Nigerian Art. Other lecture topics on more broadly based subjects like 'The Material culture of Nigeria', 'Arts and Crafts of Nigeria', 'Pottery in Nigeria' etc. are being elaborated to supplement school lessons, using materials and resources available in the museum. On a wider scale, activities take the following shapes:

- guided tours to visiting groups. Here the size of each group may vary but not exceed twenty persons. This arrangement makes it easy for museum guides to handle each group effectively; it is also deliberate policy to discourage groups from seeing the entire museum in one visit. Teachers are usually advised to prepare their pupils before they come to the museum and ensure that each visit covers only one section, prehaps relevant to a particular school lesson, that the class would like to learn about.
- illustrated lectures with slides and films in the museum education lecture theatre.
- a special holiday programme during the July to September period. This programme has become very popular with students during the holidays.
- weekly art club for children and students as part of the youth programme. Activities include painting, knitting, sculpture, modelling, adire-tie and dye techniques, drama, dress-making and weaving on the

handloom. The club also organizes excursion tours to places of interest and an exhibition of its work once a year. Film shows feature and demonstrations of how to play the traditional talking drum have become an interesting aspect of the programme. Membership is drawn from school children in an around the Lagos area. In the National Museum, Jos, the club has also become very popular. Various activities in the line with the Lagos programme are organized. Club activities are shown on television during the programme *Children's Time*.

- temporary exhibitions in the museum and in the schools with museum objects and materials supplied by schools which aim at encouraging schools to borrow museum materials for short classroom exhibitions.
- workshops, discussions and seminars in the museum for teachers and students.

Recently, a new programme for adults and other interested persons was started in the museum. In the form of a study-group on Nigerian history, Nigerian art and Nigerian culture, the programme draws members from various walks of life and of different nationalities. The majority are not Nigerians. It has become a very successful project and more and more people wish to join. The group meets weekly for two and a half hours. The aim of the project is to enable participants to learn more about Nigeria, her arts and crafts, involving active participation by all members of the group. Every member is assigned a topic of his or her choice, and uses facilities in the museum library for research, preparing the slides he would like to use and selecting a film to illustrate the topic discussed. At the end of each presentation, the group discusses the topic. Thus all participants are actively involved in positive discussion. The group so far, has covered a variety of topics including Nigerian traditional hairstyles, handloom weaving, beads in Nigeria and more serious subjects such as Nigerian art, Nigerian musical instruments and masks from the Riverine areas, etc. Excursions are organized and visits have been made to such places as Ile-Ife with its archaeological sites and Oshogbo with the Mbari houses and the Oshun Groove. Further excursions have been planned to the Rock caves in Jos Plateau, dye pits in Kano, the pottery and leather village in Naruguta, Jos and the Rock Paintings at

Geji. An interesting feature of the group is its intimacy and informality - members invite the group to hold sessions in their homes from time to time. Such 'Home Sessions' have tended to inject a new dimension into museum education activities.

One recent activity is the building up of a well-equipped audio-visual unit in the education wing, including projectors for both 16 mm films and slides, and a fairly good stock of films and slides which are used regularly in the museum and schools and which are loaned to schools on request. There are also tapes and tape-recorders and a cinema-van for out-door activities has been acquired. It is programmed to tour various parts of Nigeria, especially where there are no museums. A Mobile Museum Bus has been converted to be used for temporary exhibitions in the Lagos Museum - its extreme age ruled out further travel.

Collaboration between the museum and the school

The museum should not compete with the school. Rather it should serve as a complement to and an extension of the learning process. To ensure that 'another school' is not created in the museum, a flexible system has been evolved whereby museum education staff collaborates with teachers and students on museum education projects. Teachers are involved in discussions and planning most projects and exhibitions, although the initiative is generally the museum's.

Collaboration with schools also extends to universities and some voluntary organizations, i.e. the Nigerian

National Museum Society. In 1972 for instance, a Seminar for Teachers of History on *'Archaeology and Teaching of Nigerian History'* in the University of Ibadan was organized with the latter society. In 1975, the Ahmadu Bello University in Zaria collaborated in organizing a Seminar on *Museology in Nigeria*. There are also strong links with Institutes of African Studies in all Nigerian Universities. In August 1976, a very successful workshop for teachers and teachers-in-training on *The Role of the Museum in Education - The Nigerian Experiment* was organized with the collaboration of colleges and primary schools in the Lagos area, as part of the specialized programme for teachers and student-teachers; it greatly strengthened the link between the museum and the school. The main objectives of the workshop were to familiarize teachers with available educational resources in the museum; to enable teachers and teachers-in-training have a first hand opportunity for discussing the museum as a resource centre; and to explore the possibility of using museum objectives as effective visual aids and useful apparatus in teaching certain subjects in schools.

A new element was introduced in the workshop; participants were sent into the museum stores to select objects and mount a simple exhibition in the conference room themselves. It turned out to be an exciting exercise, generating a lively discussion among participants as each group reported on its exhibition.

Another area of collaboration with schools involves helping them set up local school museums on request. The only one so far in the country is at the Government Craft School in Pankshin, Plateau State, and it has proved very successful. Students are encouraged to bring exhibit materials from their various localities and to try to involve local people in the activities of their museum. To supplement the collections, the Lagos National Museum helps them with some objects and offers technical advice on how to set up and run a museum and introduce eductional programmes therein. It also trains staff from the school for them. However, it is stressed to the school authorities that the school museum should be a 'school affair' whereby the museum is run by the school and the exhibits planned and mounted by the students, leaving the national museum with an essentially advisory role. So far this has been a very successful project as the local people see it as 'our museum' and the students of the Advanced Teachers College in Pankshin now use the museum regularly both for research and for art lessons. It is hoped that more schools and colleges will in due course follow the 'Pankshin experiment'.

As part of the educational services, the Lagos National Museum sends out a variety of information materials - i.e. brochures on its activities, leaflets and mimeography copies of lectures and talks given both in the museum and in the school by museum staff, as well as information concerning collections of films and slides which schools are encouraged to borrow. Contact with schools is maintained through telephone calls, personal contact and circular letters. The national museum has started to receive feed back from schools, in most cases offering very useful suggestions in certain areas on how best the museum can organize some of its programmes. This is a very welcome development in its relationship with schools and colleges.

Staff and Training

All National and local museums are administered by one department - the Federal Department of Antiquities - which includes other specialized divisions like Ethnography, Archaeology Monuments and Architecture, Audio-Visual and Film Research and Curatorial Services Unit. All these units work closely together to produce a smooth system. The Museum Education Unit monitors the activities of all the units and provides the public, schools and colleges with information emanating from them.

The Education Unit, like other specialized units of the department, is staffed by professionals who are essentially university graduates with some teaching experience, although there are technical officers working in the unit too. At present, the unit has four Museum Education Officers, one Assistant Museum Education Officer and two Technical Officers as well as other supporting staff.

Most staff is trained on the job, but short intensive in-service courses are occasionally arranged for them. Study-visits are organized on the basis of attachment to museums abroad. There is a well-defined training scheme whereby every staff member in the education wing is given some training.

Problems

As the unit is still young, there are understandably some problems, particularly in the following areas:

Budget: it is insufficient to meet the needs of the programmes and therefore activities are streamlined from time to time. This constraint has also affected expected expansion? Nonetheless, available resources are utilized as best they can be and a budget increase is expected.

Staff: the unit is short-staffed at the moment but efforts are being made to recruit more qualified personel.

Space has been a long-standing problem - there is not enough space for the various activities; however, a new block will soon be completed that will house the unit properly.

Co-operation and collaboration with schools and other institutions was a serious problem some time ago, but more recently there has been some improvement in this sphere. Through various activities, there has been some success establishing a 'bridge-head' with schools, and efforts in this direction will be increased in the coming year.

Transport and Equipment are still not provided for schools wishing to visit the museum, due to a lack of vehicles (the unit has one Volkswagon bus). Audio-visual materials and other equipment generally are being built up and a Resource Unit in the museum education wing will hopefully be created.

The Future

By and large, museum education in Nigeria has taken off positively, although there remains a lot to do if more schools and people are to utilize the educational resources available in the museum. Educational planners are constantly reminded of the need to involve the museum in educational planning, especially in areas of curriculum development. This is one problem not yet solved in Nigeria. So far, a master-plan is being worked on for the Museum Education Unit to extend its services to other parts of the country, especially areas where there are no museums, and to establish the unit in all museums as soon as resources and the staff situation improve. This means establishing education services in some sixteen museums. Conferences and seminars are being organized with a view to creating more awareness among people, teachers, schools, and educational authorities of the relevance and the usefulness of museums to the educational system.

Over the years, a 'Communications Channel' has been established between the museum and the schools in the Lagos area allowing regular contacts with teachers in charge of co-ordinating museum activities in their schools and providing feed back on some of museum activities and programmes for schools.

So far, the education wing is firmly established in the National Museum at Lagos and Jos and Education Officers have just been posted to start similar programmes in Benin, Oron and Kaduna.

The involved staff members are aware that the museum as an institution has a vital role to play in Nigeria's rapidly-changing educational system, in terms of both scope and content. There will be an increase in demand for their services and they look to the future with confidence and determination. At the same time, they continue to build up expertise and resources thereby improving their ability to serve their audience more effectively and positively.

Portugal

Carmo Cabral Campos

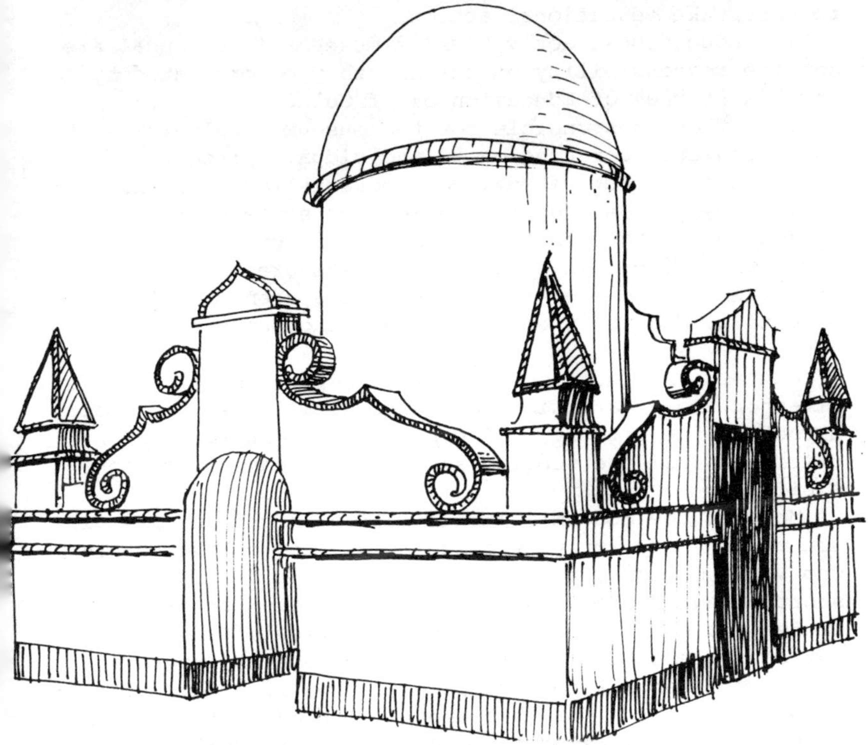

If we examine the educational activities of Portugese museums, we find that a 'movement' which has been developing over the past twenty-five years is reaching maturity thanks to the interest and perseverance of a group which followed in the footsteps of a great museologist, Dr João Couto of the *Museu Nacional de Arte Antiga**. Couto had already realized at that time the social role museums could play, he used to take his pupils and the children from the old streets of the neighbourhood to play in the museum to get them used to going in there. As he put it, adults were a lost

* National Museum of Classical Art

cause, and the activity of museums had to be rethought. He gathered together a group of young people who shared his views. Many museum directors in Portugal have not understood his message, but some do have a keen desire to undertake educational action.

The educational activities of museums in Portugal are not the responsibility of nor are they co-ordinated by the Ministeries of Education or of Culture. However, some of those responsible for the museums' cultural work have been collaborating on an individual, piecemeal basis in these activities, and requests for financial assistance can be made to a number of state bodies.

Education staff in museums do not belong to a particular profession, in spite of the pressure that has been exerted and the efforts that have been made in that direction. Most of them are dependent on uncertain budgets.

A museum's educational activity depends solely on its director and great number of responsibilities involved: directing the activity and coping with sometimes harsh criticism from the public, as well as financial responsibility.

Most of the museum's participating in the enquiry did not mention any activity based on a study of the people who visit museums, and in my view this is a serious shortcoming. There is not a single sociologist or psychologist among the staffs. However, in view of the need for an evaluation of activities which are in progress, it seems essential to undertake a study of museum visitors, albeit of a somewhat empirical kind. For this purpose the assistance of sociologists and psychologists is needed, but on a temporary basis.

The ministeries seem unaware of the services which could be rendered - by museums and other cultural institutions which could easily be set up at a regional or local level - in terms of documentation and the ability to enrich people's lives. They are also unaware of the individual interest which many museum professionals bring to this kind of activity.

The first faults, resulting from instability, are the absence of any co-ordination, the amateurishness and the perpetual experimentation.

Contact between the museum and the public is made at local level, very often through individual initiative; this can be extremely beneficial, however, since it avoids the excessive planning and centralization that

that would be introduced by a national body, whether a ministry or some other organization.

There are still museums in Portugal whose activities are not at all aimed at the public. Where educational activity does exist, it is because the directors have heard about it, but it is not generally adapted to their public. Finally, numerous curators still believe that the monumental 'tomb-museum' reserved for a privileged élite still has its place in this day and age.

There is no level of teaching at which it is planned, recommended, indicated or even suggested that museums might be used as sources of documentation or cultural enrichment. In this respect, small communities offer advantages, including closer relations among the people who live in the area. The oral tradition is kept alive.

Nonetheless, groups of teachers have become aware of the change that is going on in foreign, and even Portugese, museums, even if they are still often confronted by old museums 'done up in new packaging', as Hugues de Varine-Bohan nicely puts it.

Collaboration between museums and teaching is none the less on the increase, as a result of the experience gained in contacts between teachers and the museums; its scope is, however, sharply restricted by the fact that no specific funds are set aside for class visits to museums, even though they figure on its programme.

This collaboration is largely the result of individual initiatives.

In the field of information too there is no official liaison with the museums. No television programmes are scheduled, and the same holds true for radio. The press, which is very divided politically, does nothing to awaken people's interest in cultural matters, and none of the museums themselves contribute regular features. Publicity of this kind, though, would reach a very wide public.

Museums explain their educational aims

This article is based on a survey covering state museums and some municipal museums as well. The following passages have been selected from the replies received.

Museu de Alberto Sampaio (Guimarães). The director, a young woman with considerable personality, wrote 'The experiments we have done here have been short-lived for lack of staff. I have to cope with the administration and all the activities on my own.

'Between February and July 1976, students from the Civic Service (an experimental national service organization for students who are going on to university) took part in the experiments, and this was an enriching experience. We worked for a very varied public: (a) schools and colleges - preparatory grades in lycées, technical colleges and teacher training colleges; (b) children between 3 and 15 from different schools in the neighbourhood; and (c) cultural associations.

'For the schoolchildren, we organized guided tours to teach them to see. After these visits, we organized drawing sessions in the museum's rooms. We also went to a forge very near the museum so that we could get a better understanding of an object we had seen there.

'The work with children from the little streets around the museum has been more continuous. Wednesday is the day children come without prior enrolment to explore the museum and do painting. On thursdays another group of between fifteen and twenty children do plays. In 1976, they put on a play themselves, and did the costumes as well. They did it for the first of May and for another festival, in the square near the museum and in a cloisters belonging to the municipality.

'Contacts are now being made with retired people in order to conserve the traditions, customs and other witnesses of the past. There are also film shows in the museum.

'Collaboration has begun with the local cultural centres to put on joint activities: concerts by musical groups; an exhibition on working with linen in the municipal library; an exhibition on the popular feast of Saint Nicholas, which is traditionally celebrated by the students, in collaboration with former pupils of the lycées; and a study of leather-preparing - a speciality of the town - undertaken with the help of workers from a factory.'

Museu de Carlos Machado (Ponta Delgado, Azores). In the Azores resources may be limited, but people do all they can to turn them to account. Thus the director described activities undertaken since 1975:

'The museum has a very varied collection ranging from sixteenth-century painting to crustacea, insects and other objects. Permanent exhibitions have been mounted, and others have come from Lisbon. 'Kits' have been received from the *Museu Nacional de Arte Antiga*.

In connection with the festivals held on the Island of Santa Maria the director organized two travelling exhibitions - *The Fly* and *Life and usefulness of the snail* - and exhibitions of documentary photographs with a small explanatory and educational catalogue.

Several studies of poetry, local painters, ethnography, local ceramics and music have been mounted in another museum where the director is part-time and unpaid.

Angra do Heroísmo (Azores). A colleague wrote that: 'At the moment I am not working at the regional museum here. All I can tell you is what I know from my visits as a Friend of the Museum and what I read in the newspapers. There is a kind of museum bus which travels about on the island. There is a temporary exhibition hall where lycée pupils go for visual education. I know of no education service.'

Leiria. The director of the museum in this small town in central Portugal, wrote: 'Unfortunately I am waiting for the museum to get new facilities, and so am unable to have any cultural programme. I feel constrained but I am determined to nurture a love of art and history in students, of whom very large numbers visit the museum. They say I help them: that is important in this miserable museum.'

Nazaré. This is one of the most charming of Portugal's fishing beaches. One is struck by the beauty of the landscape and the way the women are dressed. Here one can still believe in romantic medieval legends. But the cultural isolation of Nazaré is very great, hence the local museum's intention to fill some of the gaps once it has the necessary audio-visual equipment, which will be forthcoming due to the joint initiatives of teachers and students. Obviously the programme will have to be established with particular concern for their adaptation to the environment in which they are to be used.

The museum's aim is to make known and to develop local culture as a meeting point for broadening cultural contacts. It intends to join the group which is beginning a study of regionalization.

Lamego. This town is in the wine-growing area where port comes from. Between 1960 and 1962 the local museum carried out a curious experiment in cultural education with the local army barracks, the CIOE. Three sergeants had been trained as guides, and all the officers and men posted to Lamego learned to know the town, its very beautiful monuments and the history of the artists who lived there.

Museu-Biblioteca Conde de Castro Guimarães. (Cascais,*

a seaside resort near Lisbon). There is a workshop and a library for children and young people. The municipality provides funds, and the library, which collaborates with the schools, is becoming busier all the time. Female staff organize games, competitions, and discussions, and get the young people drawing. As interest has grown, debates have been organized on literary subjects, the theatre, etc. The staff visit the schools one day a week and, with the teachers, organize plays, marionnette shows, and story and poetry readings.

The workshop, which was started in 1964, takes fifteen children for two hours three times a week. They paint and do modelling and line engraving, as well as staging plays and going on visits to the monuments of Cascais.

Post Office Museum (Lisbon). Because it is essentially technical, the museum received a warm welcome from the general public, although it is visited mainly by school age children and the disabled. Its education service organizes a large number of guided tours: seven schools for the blind and other disabled children have been on these tours, as have three groups of retired people. Children and young people are very enthusiastic about seeing the telegraph and telephone systems in operation. (Technical museums are rare in Portugal.)

At the end of the garden, there is a pavillon called 'The Coaching Station', the front of which is covered with *azulejos* (painted ceramic tiles) recalling the means of transport used in former times. Four stage

---

* Counts of Castro Guimarães Museum and Library

coaches are on show, as well as a scale-model coaching station, uniforms and paintings on the subject of transport.

The education service organizes guided tours on the following subjects: postal service, stamps, radio, the telegraph, the telephone, and transport from the sixteenth century to the present day.

Museu Nacional dos Côches (Carriage Museum) (Lisbon). The education service of this very rare and beautiful museum has two main activities - guided tours for schools and courses for children. The education service has a full-time female organizer and two part-timers.

The courses are for groups of children aged from 4 to 6, from 7 to 8, and from 9 to 12, and are held from 3 to 5 p.m. on four consecutive Saturdays. They consist of a talk lasting about an hour, followed by a period in which the children model, draw or paint the objects which have impressed them most.

This museum is the only one of its kind in Portugal and so has a lot of visitors and it possesses a very rich collection of documents on transport, equestrian sports, uniforms, books, bull-fighting and harnesses.

Museu Nacional de Soares dos Reis (Oporto). This museum reported that: 'The museum has had an education service for sixteen years, and with its limited resources it attempts to make its riches known to the old town of Oporto and further beyond. Its staff is very small and so its activity, especially exterior, remains experimental.

'Relations between the museum and the schools are being established slowly and often at an individual level; however, this does not mean that the staff are not working hard - everyone at the moment is very busy. Resources for the activities are very rudimentary, cooperation by the staff helps overcome the difficulties. Cultural activity is aimed at (1) children; (2) young people; (3) adults.

'For *children*, there are guided tours. The theme is requested by the school, suggested by the museum or else worked out by the two together. The tour may take in the whole museum, temporary exhibitions, travelling exhibitions or small special exhibitions, organized in collaboration with the teachers to help them in their class teaching; there are also visits to the temporary exhibitions of the Centre for Contemporary Art (a body that operates within the museum).

'There is a workshop which has been in existence for sixteen years and is held three times a week for different groups (4 to 6 years, 7 to 12 years) with entrance to the museum; there is painting, collage, modelling, line engraving, experimentation with films or slides (teaseling, painting), painting of a given subject and painting a subject of one's own choice, group painting and individual painting and experiments with teachers and groups of pupils; before the session each group visits the museum to see an exhibition, a film, the garden or a mimed display and to learn about the life of the museum.

'A workshop organized by the museum operated in a railway station for two months to celebrate the centenary of the railways; there was also an exhibition of children's painting. The workshop was at the other end of town, which enabled it to reach a different section of the public.

'For training of an aesthetic or artistic nature, there are games played in the museum, historical information, mimed displays illustrating a work of art, eurhythmics, and study of one or several works of art, followed by a drawing or painting session.

'For *young people,* the museum has been organizing holiday courses since 1971 (in addition to the small special exhibitions organized in collaboration with the school staff):

1971: painting outdoors in the park.
1972: workshop and study of an important exhibition of painting.
1973: no holiday workshop.
1974: two groups of eighteen children living in a poor district near the museum.
1975: help from the Civic Service, workshop with children from the district, visits to children's hospitals and old people's homes with drawing materials and films.
1976: two groups of 14- to 16-year-olds, with free entry to the museum, study of the exhibition of contemporary art, recreational experiments in the workshop.

'During the year, there are activities for *adults* and *young people,* but they are not regular. There are musical appreciation classes; concerts; discussions of artistic trends or techniques; cinema; exhibitions organized at the museum by Friends of the Museum with pieces from their collections, under the direction of the curators; a marionnette theatre organized with young people; and study followed by an exhibition by groups of young people in the old district, near the museum (the exhibition was held in a club in the suburbs).

'As far as facilities for the physically handicapped are concerned, we have difficulties. Portugal's museums were planned without lifts or alternative means of access, and without special toilets. Furthermore, almost all museums, our own included, are housed in former palaces with several floors, which are rarely heated in winter, and this is far from ideal for the disabled who cannot walk. We regularly get handicapped children coming to the workshop along with normal children and we regard this as being of great educational value for everyone. In particular, we have deaf mutes, and they have great powers of observation and expression. For the physically handicapped who cannot walk we have installed a cinema and other facilities on the ground floor, but once again this separates them from other people.

'In my view, there have been too many experiments which have not been followed up.'

Museu Municipal 'Dr. Santos Rocha' (Figueira da Foz). When the director of this municipal museum on the coast in central Portugal was asked why there was no education service in his museum, he replied: 'The museum is closed for redecoration. However, we have collaborated with several groups of teachers who have asked for our assistance and we organize film shows twice a week. But is that what the museum public needs, and are we achieving it? I really don't think we are. It's cosmetic. I do not think that the social and economic conditions of the country enable us yet to reorganize the education services and, consequently, collaboration between the museum and the schools. It also seems to me that the museums are not yet prepared for serious work at grass-roots level, starting in a modest way but building up to something really worth while.'

Museu Nacional de Arte Antiga (Lisbon). The museum education service was started in 1978. The objectives of the museum (the education service included) concern bringing its public to critical consciousness by means of discovery and personal research.

In specific terms, there is genuine activity directed towards an interested but still relatively limited school public. There is a potential public which the museum *must* be interested in, either by seeking new methods of activity or by developing what is already within its reach.

Contacts made at the beginning of each year with the schools, local authorities, institutions and various associations in Lisbon and its suburbs, provide information about the possibilities of the museum and making suggestions about participation.

In terms of education, the museum works continuously with local primary schools and lycées, to which it can make a special contribution, benefitting the teachers as much as the pupils, by the activities carried out in the museum or the school. These include *ad hoc* visits, series of visits, and seminars. Specific activities are organized for the handicapped, particularly the blind. There are exhibitions and participation in courses for teachers.

As a back-up to special visits, there are workshops exploring certain temporary exhibitions or studying various techniques. During the summer, there is also a workshop in the garden, for activities ranging from painting to weaving, from engraving to movement or making musical instruments.

Meetings with teachers/educationists take place on request and in the context of training teachers. Courses, seminars, the development of people's sensitivities and educational research (in the museum, in the town or in the country) are also important to the museum.

The entire work of the education service is centred on continuous assessment of the activity in progress, this at the same time providing a basis for giving the museum education staff continuous in-service training.

Museu Calouste Gulbenkian. In view of the fact that schools do not have exclusive responsibility for education, and that museums are ideal places in which to awaken the aesthetic and critical senses and the knowledge of children and young people, the Gulbenkian museum has been planned and built up so as to work in conjunction with the school curricula.

As soon as the museum opened, the education service began its work by sending programmes to the schools and collaborating with them, to supplement their activities and encourage them to discover its resources.

Later, the service felt the need to take the

museum to the schools which could not come to it and the idea of a travelling exhibition was born. It consists of photographs of museum objects chosen for pupils aged between 10 and 17 in connection with the school curricula.

Other initiatives in progress include discussions of history, games of discovery at the museum, publication of *Calouste Gulbenkian and the Flying Carpet,* which tells the story of his collection and puzzles and other games involving reproducing museum objects.

As far as collaboration with the universities is concerned, the museum offers slide collections to university teachers as well as secondary school teachers; it also holds archives of slides on different themes in art and history, organized for lending to teachers; in addition, there are transport subsidies for visits to temporary exhibitions at the museum; and the curators give students assistance in their work.

Portuguese museums which have no official educational activities have many material difficulties and major problems in finding staff to organize them, since arranging such activities is not regarded as a profession. Those who do it are not on the staff and have little opportunity of getting their voices heard.

Equipment is almost non-existent. The education services, instead of taking a prominent part in extending the sphere of influence of the museums, are generally considered the poor relations. However, it is mainly the organizers of educational activities who believe in the possibilities offered by the museums and who fight for action by the whole museum team geared to the school curricula.

Thailand

Chira Chongkol

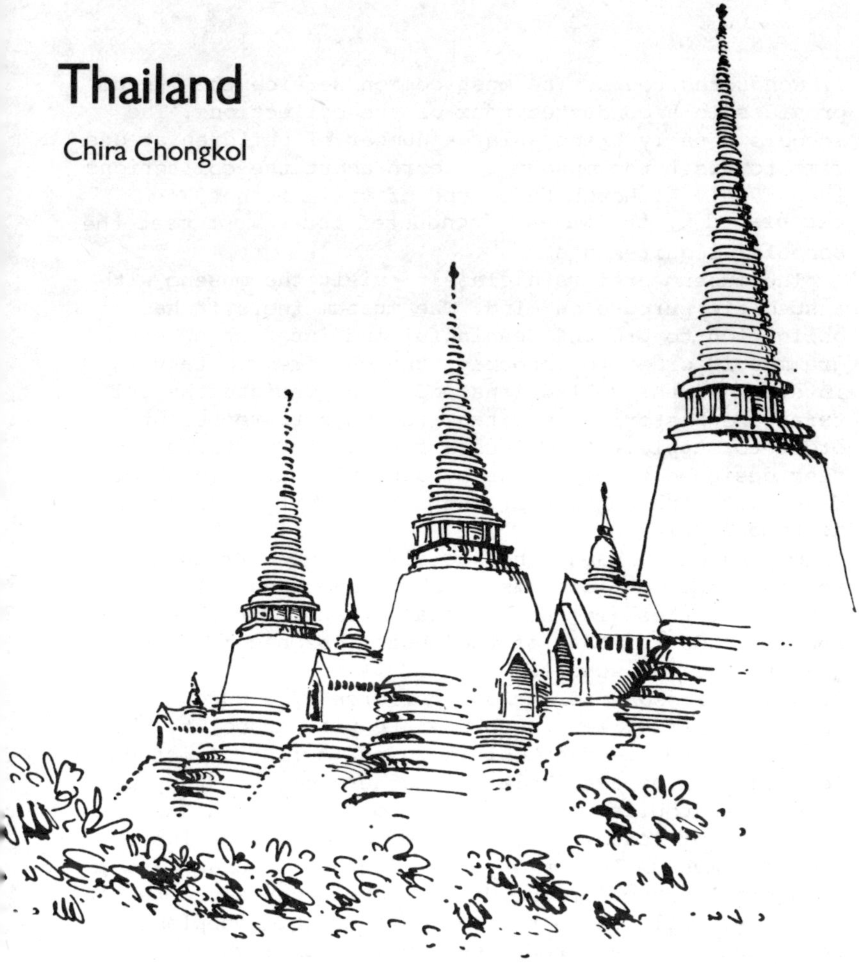

The Bangkok National Museum has provided educational services for a long time, but it was not until 1969 that an educational staff was formally established. At present, there are seven education officers to serve over 500,000 students who visit the museum annually. Education programmes for all age groups have been developed and are gradually being expanded; adult education programmes include services for foreigners.

The Bangkok National Museum serves a large number of school children at the primary and secondary levels. Routine activities include the following three programmes.

1. *Conducted tours*. The most common service the museum provides is a conducted tour of the collections. The schools usually bring a large number of children at one time to visit the museum to learn about the collections in general. Although this type of visit is not encouraged by the museum, conducted tours must meet the schools' requirements.

The museum prefers a class to visit the museum with a specific purpose in mind. The museum feels it has an obligation to present meaningful and interesting programmes in order to encourage the children to take an interest in the collections and to appreciate the cultural and historical heritage the objects represent. In order to supplement various areas of study, tours have been designed to emphasize a particular area in accordance with the context of the school curriculum or textbooks.

On the other hand, the social studies curriculum requires that children learn about important places and one of these is the National Museum. For this reason, a conducted tour of the museum has become a requisite for the schools.

2. *Museum lessons for school children*. The museum educational staff tries to co-operate with school teachers who plan for out-of-school learning. A list of museum lessons is made available to teachers so that they may select the topics most suitable to their needs and plan their out-of-school learning programmes. The value of having a museum lesson on a particular topic and involving small groups of children has been explained to the teachers. While those topics that directly supplement the texts are preferred, there are often requests for tours of additional galleries after the lesson.

3. *Special programmes for children*. The national museums in Bangkok and the provinces organize a special programme for children once a year on National Children's Day. Special exhibitions are presented, pamphlets and leaflets on museum exhibits are distributed and several types of competitive programmes and games are provided. During the summer vacation, a creative art class using volunteer teachers is provided for children from six through twelve years of age.

In order to encourage adults to visit, the Bangkok National Museum has arranged a changing exhibition gallery, where a special presentation is provided for the public every three to four months. The goal of the temporary exhibitions is to promote an understanding and appreciation of the art and culture of Thailand and to encourage the people to form the habit of making an occasional visit to the museum. Whether the exhibition is permanent or temporary, both education and personal enjoyment are taken into consideration in the presentation of museum collections.

Guided tours are provided for the general public. There are general tours of all the galleries, as well as a gallery talk on one particular gallery.

Programmes for adults have been extended to serve foreign visitors. The Bangkok National Museum has an unusual education programme based on international co-operation. A volunteer group of foreign ladies, residents of Bangkok, was founded in 1969. With the assistance of this group, the museum provides conducted tours of its collections in English, French, German and Japanese, as well as a special lecture in English for the general public each month.

A pilot project on 'Museums and Adult Education' has been in progress since 1974. As part of this project, a programme of travelling exhibitions together with educational and cultural activities was developed for rural communities in 1977. This is a joint project of the National Museum and the National Theatre. The museum educational staff arranges the exhibits and gives talks to students and the general public throughout the day, while dancing and music are presented in the evening. Travelling exhibitions have become popular, and many requests have been received from various provinces to have museum exhibition presented in their towns.

Contents and Methods

The collections of the national museums in Bangkok and in the provinces are chiefly related to art and archaeology, and include art treasures and archaeological artifacts found in Thailand.

The goal of the museum is to emphasize social and cultural values. Exhibitions are arranged so that the information presented helps the public to understand and appreciate their cultural heritage, and so wish to preserve it for future generations.

Educational activities include special exhibitions, conducted tours, gallery talks, museum lessons, film shows, lectures, excursions, creative art classes for children, a loan service, travelling exhibitions, and talks at schools.

Museum lessons are both formal and informal in their approach. These programmes are designed to be used only with small groups of pupils who come to visit the museum with a particular purpose in mind. Most of the schools, however, bring very large numbers of children at one time with no specific programme in mind, and are thus unable to request a tour of a particular area of the museum.

The museum has established a two-way communication system with the schools, whereby the schools come to the museum and the museum goes to the schools. Upon request, a museum officer will go to a school, and present a talk using audio-visual materials and some objects which the students may examine closely or even handle.

Excursions to museums, monuments, and sites are occasionally arranged for the public. For travelling exhibitions to rural communities, exhibition kits and loose objects packed in boxes, as well as photographs and slides and films, are used. These are transported by a micro-bus and a jeep.

A creative art programme that includes painting, pottery, and papier-maché is organized for children during school vacations and taught by volunteer teachers. Lessons are related to the museum collections, in that the children are taken to a particular gallery where they receive inspiration for their work, and gain an appreciation for the art works.

Excursions to monuments and museums. Excursions are specially arranged. For example, an overnight excursion to the monuments and ruins of Sukhothai, a 13th century capital city in the North, included visits to museums and monuments along the way. In the evening, a cultural programme of dancing and drama was presented. Transportation for this particular tour consisted of two air-conditioned buses.

Museum to school method. The museum receives frequent requests from the schools and its approach is always in accordance with the specific request. A museum officer may go to the school and present a talk on a particular subject using exhibits, photographs, slides, or tapes to illustrate the talk.

Travelling exhibitions. 'Travelling kits' for mobile

exhibitions to rural areas have been compiled. These kits, together with boxes of exhibit objects and audio-visual materials, are packed in an omnibus, while the education officers use a landrover. This project is organized in co-operation with the National Theatre so that a programme of both the performing art and visual arts may be presented in the provinces.

Special Potentials

Three or four special exhibitions are arranged each year in the Bangkok National Museum. A handbook of each exhibition is published. These changing exhibitions are supplemented by a lecture and a special presentation for children using audio-visual material. If the topic concerns excavation, a film or a slide show on excavations will be shown. Talks may include the handling of artifacts.

A special programme for Buddhist monks on the occasion of Buddhist Lent is unique to Thailand as a Buddhist country. Each year, during the first week of Buddhist Lent, a special exhibition is arranged, and a handbook published for presentation to the monks. The museum arranges two days of special programmes and monks from all over the country are invited to visit the museum. Between 10,000 and 15,000 Buddhist monks visit the museum each year.

Museum officers encourage students to collect various objects and teachers are advised to set up museums at their schools.

One example of the way museum collections are used

for education is a special show entitled, 'Archaeological Dance and Archaeological Costumes'. The curators studied period costumes and dance gestures of the sculpture from the different historical periods in the museum collections. In co-operation with the School of Dramatic Art, costumes and dance movements which corresponded to the sculpture were devised and presented to the public on the occasion of the 20th Anniversary celebration of ICOM. Eighty students from the School of Dramatic Art paraded in their costumes inside the museum compound, and dances of the different periods were performed. A publication on the costumes was printed. This programme is still popular, and school students in general like to perform the archaeological dances and model the period costumes. There are frequent requests from schools to borrow sets of these costumes.

A music and drama festival lasting one week during the cool season is performed in the museum compound. Three months of weekend music programmes from March through May follow this festival.

In its development of school curriculum the education authority has invited the museum to send officers to serve on its working committees. This is an encouraging trend for closer co-operation between the museum and the Ministry of Education.

Organization of Museum Educational Activities

Museum educational activities in Thailand have been initiated by the museum itself. There has been no pressure from any institution nor from the public for the museum to provide such services. However, such services as the museum has provided have been met with favourable response from both the schools and the general public.

As previously mentioned, the Museum Volunteer Group of foreign ladies has been very active in organizing activities. They present well-organized conducted tours of the museum collections in various foreign languages, arrange for open public lectures in English once a month by a Thai or foreign scholar, and organize special excursions to monuments and museums throughout Thailand. A special course for foreigners on an introduction to the traditional art of Thailand is presented twice a year by members of this volunteer group. This course has become very popular as foreign residents in Bangkok find it quite useful.

The Role of the Museum Staff and School Teachers

The Bangkok National Museum has a special staff of four graduate personnel and three assistants in charge of educational services. The school curriculum in Thailand does not require many out-of-school activities, which makes it difficult to offer museum lessons to the schools. Teachers generally prefer conducted tours primarily concerned with the history and art of the later periods. They fail to attach much importance to either prehistory or the early historical periods, which they consider only as archaeological exhibitions beyond the pupils' understanding. The museum staff has tried to help teachers to understand all of the collections so that they might be able to make use of them.

A lecture course on art and archaeology in Thailand has been provided for school teachers of different levels during the summer vacation. This introductory course, which included excursions to museums, monuments, and sites, was organized in co-operation with the Department of General Education. Social studies' teachers were selected to take the course. The lecturers included information on the history of art in Thailand and on important exhibits in the museum. They also provided guidelines on how to make use of the museum for educational purposes. The programme was successful - teachers found the course helpful and continue to keep in touch with the museum staff when they plan their school visits to the museum. They also make use of other museum services by inviting museum officers to give talks on particular topics at the schools, and requesting loan collections and audio-visual materials on museum collections. In addition, information sheets and leaflets on different aspects of the museum collections are made available to the teachers.

Information

The ICOM National Committee in Thailand has published a museum directory in Thailand, and provincial and site museums have guidebooks to their collections on sale. Brochures of programmes for foreigners are prepared by the Volunteer Group.

There are mimeographed leaflets on museum services for schools, and the education staff prepares mimeographed newsletters for distribution. There are also information sheets and leaflets on different topics of the museum collections, and handbooks of each temporary exhibition are on sale.

The schools may contact the museum by letter requesting a tour or lesson, or telephone for an appointment with an education officer. Museum staff members are sometimes invited to participate in seminars and panel discussions organized by educational institutions.

Problems and Future Plans

Full co-operation between the museum and the schools is still quite difficult to attain. As previously mentioned, the museum prefers pupils to come to the museum well prepared by their teachers, and with a particular purpose in mind so that they can take full advantage of their visit.

One of the problems in Thailand is that the contribution museums can make to education has been largely overlooked. The educational authorities have failed to consider the informal learning which the museum can provide to both children and adults as part of the educational process. Moreover, educational and cultural programmes are limited by inadequate financing for equipment and personnel. In spite of this, the museum has tried to initiate ways in which it can contribute as much as possible to education, establish a close working relationship between museums and education agencies, and continue to improve its own standards.

Plans for future activities of the museum will be concerned with lifelong education. It is through its activities that the museum will be able to bring people to the museum, as well as take the museum to people through its travelling exhibitions and outside programmes. One future project involves a museum travelling bus. The methods employed in working with people in both the urban and the rural areas are proving to be effective. The museum is, however, in need of additional support from the government, if it is to provide good services and work in an efficient manner to fulfill its functions and responsibilities to the community and to the general public.

Union of Soviet Socialist Republics

V. Tyazhelov and others

Collaboration with schools occupies an important place among the various activities of Soviet museums. Children are the most frequent museum visitors. Although museums direct their activities towards pupils in secondary schools and institutions of technical and specialized secondary education, including the apprenticeship schools, recently collaboration with pre-school institutions has been greatly extended.

Museum educational activities have common features inspired by the State's education aims as well as specific features determined by the cultural and national traditions of the peoples of the U.S.S.R. and the nature of the collections involved themselves. Museum activities are also shaped by the initiative of the individual staffs. It is not easy to include all this rich experience in a short report, and for that reason this paper will deal only with the principal forms of collaboration between Soviet museums and schools.

Soviet museums organize their educational activities with due regard to the general aims of education, as understood in the State, and their own particular bent. In working out their detailed plans for public education, museums naturally take into account school curricula as well as the ages and intellectual levels of their young visitors. They do not consider their role as merely complementing lessons by illustrating them, thereby playing a secondary role. Each museum, depending on its nature and specialization, seeks to broaden and deepen pupils' knowledge, finding its own themes and points of contact with the school audience, while bearing in mind the lessons to be learnt from pedagogical science. The fine arts museums put the main emphasis on aesthetic education through the medium of the plastic arts in order to give young visitors their first idea of the essential features of different genres and types of work and to tell them something of the history of art. The literary museums draw the attention of their young visitors to documents illustrating the process of artistic creation; they import a historical view of literary creation without ignoring problems of an aesthetic nature. The museums of science and technology help pupils in their future professional careers.

The guided tour is the commonest museum activity and enables a large number of pupils to get to know the collection. The themes and composition of the guided tours depend on the particular nature of the museum and can be very diverse. They may be general and cover the entire collection, or have a specific theme and show only objects illustrating that theme. Guided tours of this kind either take place on one single occasion or form a cycle. The length of the tour and the complexity of the material being studied depend on the age of the visitors.

The fine arts museums present pupils with the objects that correspond to the literature, history or art curricula (from 7 to 13 years of age); in some schools, there are special courses in fine arts. The literary museums devote lectures for school students to literary periods, or the work of a particular writer, or even the genesis of a particular work. The technical museums take account of the physics, chemistry and mathematics curricula. The Polytechnical Museum in Moscow organizes several guided tours which enable different school subjects to be studied solely through the objects exhibited in the museum. The activities of the museums of music enable the problems of aesthetic education to be tackled in a broader perspective than is possible in the schools.

In addition to tours linked in one way or another to the school curriculum, most museums develop methods of initiating pupils into the various aspects of technological culture of artistic creation. They organize various types of competition, concerts, cycles of more detailed guided tours, evenings and meetings held in co-operation with other interested bodies such as the Ministry of Public Education and the arts unions. Pupils go to the history museums and the memorial museums to celebrate important dates and to come into contact with famous people of the time.

In addition to guided tours, museums also offer their visitors a large number of lectures. This permits a freer choice than is possible during the guided tour of the scientific material being studied, and encourages a greater diversity of lecture subjects. There are lecture centres located close to the museums specifically for school students. The museum staff also gives lectures in the schools with the aid of slides, records and tapes. Museums which have cinemas show educational and scientific films which are within the understanding of everyone; in certain of the museums of literature the works of famous writers are screened. Schools are sent travelling exhibitions of prints, reproductions and sometimes even original pictures.

Interest groups and study circles organized for children form an important part of museum activities and it is the museums that take the initiative in this field. Near the State Hermitage Museum in Leningrad and the State Pushkin Museum of Fine Arts in Moscow, there are drawing studies for children between 4 and 10 years of age. They use the museum collections for educational and instructional purposes. But as a general rule the interest groups linked to museums are for children between 12 and 17 years of age. The State Hermitage Museum, the State Pushkin Museum of Fine Arts and the State Russian Museum have considerable experience in this field. However, the methods used by other museums are sometimes original and are also well worth looking at. The groups or circles, organized for pupils aged 12 to 14, relate more to the school curriculum and the work resembles a lesson, albeit a rather special kind of lesson since it is held in the presence of objects on show in a museum. Added to that is the active assimilation on the part of the members of the circle; they give talks and make reports, build models, put on plays, make costumes and paint scenery. Members of archaeological circles take part in digs, make brief trips to excavation sites and follow their progress. For senior classes, courses are organized which involve a free choice of the subject and the method of presenting the material; lecture series and practical work (in seminars) are associated. Senior pupils often do their summer courses of practical work in the museums. For schoolboys and schoolgirls who are involved, the museums organize free coach trips to the sights and historic places in the various towns, as well as meetings with painters and visits to their studios, thay can also visit the museum or workshop library.

Numerous schools in towns and villages throughout the country are 'adopted' by museums. The museums organize travelling exhibitions and centres which offer advice and present their collections, and assist in the organization and running of museum sections attached to schools. This kind of activity is associated both with museums in large towns and with local museums. Staff members of large museums who give lectures all over the country -- a practice which has developed a great deal recently -- are also available to advise the pupils and answer their questions.

From the museum side, collaboration with individual schools is carried out through special sections or centres or with the assistance of staff members who assume this responsibility. Their job consists of working out, in conjunction with the museum administration and the scientific sections, the specific forms which educational activity will take. They have to co-ordinate their work with the public education officials and maintain contacts with the schools. The museums of the Soviet Union -- and first and foremost the major museums which have a sizeable staff -- prepare methodological guidelines to govern their educational activities, drawing on the results of psycho-sociological studies of children's perception in museums. The most representative group of research workers in this field is currently working at the State Russian Museum in Leningrad. Some questions concerning collaboration between museums and schools are discussed during lectures and meetings held at national level. To draw up the plans for educational work the museums consult with the U.S.S.R. Academy of Pedagogical Sciences, the Union and Republic Ministries of Public Education and the authorities responsible for education and in-service training for teachers in the main cities. This enables programmes to be modified and improved and courses, seminars and lectures to be organized for the teaching staff of the schools and pre-school institutions.

The museums are often at the origin of these contacts. Account is taken of the experience of the museums in writing some chapters in textbooks: for example, the chapter on the plastic arts in history books. The museums of fine arts, the Academy of Pedagogical Sciences, the Academy of Arts of the U.S.S.R., and the Union of U.S.S.R. Artists are in the process of working out a joint programme of aesthetic education. Some museums have preliminary discussions with the teachers regarding new themes for lectures and visits.

The museums have special rooms for work with school students, as well as special libraries and reproduction facilities. For security reasons, in fine arts museums it is forbidden to use the original objects outside the exhibition. In the technical museums on the other hand, it is desirable and in some cases compulsory for work with school students to make use of appropriate equipment (machine-tools, machinery, apparatus, collections of minerals). Some museums arrange for their study groups or circles to visit laboratories and restorers' workshops. The staff who are concerned with this educational work are chosen from specialists with diplomas in higher education.

Only students in faculties of art have a course in a museum prescribed as part of their programme of study. Museums whose staff have no training as teachers train personnel for the purpose with their own resources. They employ teachers or send their specialists to staff training courses organized by the ministries and authorities which they come under.

As well as informing the schools of their activities through brochures, manuals, and posters or announcements on the radio and in the newspapers, the museum staff also approach teachers and other educational personnel directly. As far as enterprises are concerned, they receive written invitations, but this does not exclude telephone contacts and other forms of communication.

The brochures, programmes and prospectuses concern the activities of a single museum in general. The list giving guided tours and lecture subjects is accompanied by brief notes which enable the school authorities to make their choice. There are also posters announcing temporary exhibitions in different museums and exhibition halls. The initiative for this publicity belongs to the museums, but they are able to count on the help of the schools and in-service training institutes, which remain in permanent contact with them.

United Kingdom of Great Britain and Northern Ireland

Victoria Airey

In the United Kingdom there are some 900 museums, including national, provincial* and private institutions. Varying provision is made for education work in those institutions: some eighty-four museum education services as such exist, with staff ranging from thirty in Cardiff to a single museum education officer working on his own but in co-operation with the museum's curatorial staff in many smaller establishments. In addition, many other

* National museums are financed by the Government and their employees are civil servants; provincial museums include all other non-private institutions, financed by local authorities, companies, etc.

museums provide some educational facilities through the work of curatorial staff. Most of these services have developed in England (about seventy-five); in Scotland there are eleven, in Northern Ireland two, and in Wales there is the comprehensive service provided by the National Museum of Wales plus two other services.

The first museum education service began in Liverpool in 1872 with a loan service; an education service was set up in Glasgow in 1918; following the encouragement given by the British Association and the Museums Association, together with Carnegie United Kingdom Trust reports by Sir Henry Miers in 1928 and S.F. Markham in 1938, a number of museum education services was set up before the Second World War - notably in Leicestershire (Carnegie-assisted) and in Derbyshire where a Carnegie grant enabled Barbara Winstanley to start her loan service both of museum items and later of audio-visual hardware and software under the auspices of the Local Education Authority*.

During the period immediately after the Second World War, the development of further museum education services got off to a slow start. The Rosse Report of the Standing Commission on Provincial Museums and Galleries (1963) was responsible for the wave of newly established departments started in the sixties. An important Department of Education and Science report on Museum Education, a Schools Council Report of the early 1970s *Pteradactyls and Old Lace* (103), the Wright Report (1973) and local government reorganization of 1974 should almost have completed an even spread of services throughout England, but economic circumstances began at this time to overtake plans. Only those authorities which created new posts very early during the period were actually able to get further departments off the ground.

The growth of the museum education movement in this country has occurred gradually over almost a century, and owes its origin both to individual enthusiasm and

---

* *Local Education Authority (LEA):* A county or metropolitan district authority responsible for the administration of educational establishments in their area, for finance, for the employment of staff, and for the organization or partial organization of support services and advisory services. The Authority is headed by a Chief Education Officer.

to official reports urging museums to look both at general education potential and, in particular, at the potential for formal education in the form of schools, teachers and children. The nineteenth century concept of museums stressed their importance for popular education. Indeed, the Victoria and Albert Museum (V and A) was founded with just this in mind. In 1919 there was an unsuccessful move to bring museums under the responsibility of the Local Education Authorities. The V and A circulating exhibitions department was founded in the late nineteenth century in order to bring national collections to people throughout the country. The V and A also established a central purchasing fund for provincial museums to draw on; this example was followed by the Science Museum in 1973, on the recommendation of the Wright Report. Thus provincial museums were able to make important and expensive purchases. But despite these general trends, and important as they are, the tendency until the 1960s had been to regard museum education in the United Kingdom as museum schools services. The Group for Educational Services in Museums (GESM), started in the early 1950s by a nucleus of museum education officers as 'The Group for Children's Activities in Museums', was renamed only in 1963.

With the encouragement of the Wright Report and of the Museums Association document 'Museums in Education', however, new services began to be set up specifically as Education Services with wider responsibility and potential. Since the sixties museum education officers have had a much wider role in developing and contributing towards adult education and the education potential of the museum as a whole as well as their traditional role of museum schools officers. In 1973 the GESM committee became the British national education committee for ICOM and more cross currents of ideas and information than ever before are now flowing through international conferences, exchange study tours (Anglo-Belgian 1975-78), newsletters (*Market of Ideas Bulletin* edited in Stockholm) and contacts between formally organized groups of museum education officers in various countries. These international developments too have highlighted the broad educational potential of museums; and the museum profession as a whole in the United Kingdom increasingly recognizes, accepts and co-operates in forwarding the educational aims of museums. In 1975, GESM held an international conference in London to look at future developments in museum education.

The foundation of museum education services during the century has by no means been uniform. Some of the reasons for their development have already been explained; and to some extent their varied roles have been conditioned by the terms of their foundation as well as by the individuals who have built them up. The national museums have tended to develop as teaching and advisory services, both for teachers and children; in the provinces loan services to schools have been of equal, or sometimes greater importance, than teaching and advisory services, particularly those based on a county museum with a widely scattered rural population to serve. A number of services, particularly in the early sixties, followed the early lead of the Derbyshire - the Local Education Authority founded and financed them largely to provide loan and advisory services, and housed them outside museums. Museums in the area could not provide such services for themselves. Such provision was started before the concept of resource centres or teachers' centres* came into being in this country.

While there is then no common course of development in museum education, various common patterns can be traced.

Today most Local Education Authorities have a number of support services** on which schools, teachers and

---

* *Teachers' Centres:* Centres for in-service training for teachers, and often used as a social centre too. Audio-visual equipment is often loaned from such a base, and other material such as films and other teaching resources may be available too. The teachers' centre usually has a very good stock of reference material about local support services, library books, text books, etc. and acts generally as an information clearing house.

** *Support Services:* in each county or metropolitan district or other unit area of local government, there are a number of back-up services in education, which may or may not be wholly or partly responsible to the Education Authority. Such services include Teachers' Centres, Library Service, Museum Education Service, Radio and Television Education Services, Theatre Education Services, Archives Education Services, Field Study Centres, Resource Centres, Health Education Services, etc.

children can rely for the very flexible learning processes used. In addition, in most areas of the country non-LEA support can be expected from the Forestry Commission, Nature Conservancy Council, the National Trust, Archives Offices, Naturalists' Trusts, the Directorate of Ancient Monuments and Historic Buildings of the Department of the Environments, etc. There is a very rich network for the teacher to draw on in order to study the environment, both in terms of expertise and material resources prepared for them in the form of documents, photographs, maps, slides, films and educational packs in general. It is therefore common practice for the museum education officer to be in touch with all such relevant organizations in his own area - either to give or receive help to pool resources, or to be able to advise teachers and student teachers where else they can go for help with a particular project. Derbyshire LEA, for example, has managed to pool a number of its educational resources in a remarkable way: the county museum's officer is one of three members of the management group of the schools resources services which embraces a museum schools loan section, a schools library section, a picture loan service to schools and the loan of audio-visual hardware and software. Schools can therefore select a number of loan resources through one centre as well as obtaining expert advice on any relevant fields of information, as well as technical help. In Yorkshire seven Local Education Authorities have formed a Consortium which shares a school museum and resource service covering loan collections and the Clarke Hall Educational Museum, a 17th century farmer's house. This shared service is available to over 2,000 schools and colleges. Within the region, a number of other museum services, centred in the major cities, provide valuable local loan services and intra-mural educational activities in their museums.

There is considerable interaction between different institutions; two which commonly work quite closely together are libraries amd museums - loaning books for a teaching project or loaning museum specimens for a book display. A museum might hold an in-service course for teachers at a teachers' centre, while a museum education officer might also write a child-centred learning project on, for example, *Fossils* for a resources-for-learning centre.

Local Education Authorities sometimes have complete

or part administrative and financial control over museum education services; the museum education service tends usually to form one section of a whole series of support services. Courses, teaching programmes, loans and advisory services are sometimes the result of teachers' own ideas, sometimes of interaction between local support services, or perhaps the result of a radio or television series for schools, or a national exhibition, a national or even international event. Exhibitions which have drawn national and international crowds to London in the last few years have included the Tutankhamun, Chinese, and Pompeii collections. During the year of the Tutankhamun exhibition, provincial museums with Egyptology Collections were crowded with visiting school groups. One such museum in Leicester organized in-service training courses for local teachers, presenting them with ideas for preparation, museum visits and follow-up work, so that they were then self-sufficient to use the museum's resources.

It is noticeable that while a museum often offers a teaching programme or project in compliance with schools' wishes or a subject of current importance, equally teachers often look to the museum for inspiration. One such project begun by the schools service at Bristol City Museum has been the Avon Educational Cruises: the museum and a local steamship company have together organized these: in-service courses are held for teachers in local teachers' centres where talks on various aspects of environmental studies potential are given - for instance, on the industrial archaeology, natural history and geology of the region; a film is shown by the Port of Bristol Authority and essential information given about the ship, safety drills etc. Information packs are given to teachers and a display of books and other resources enables them also to pick up ideas for preparing their pupils. When the cruises are held, commentary is kept down to a minimum; children work on pre-prepared worksheets at some stages of the journey, but they also enjoy exploring the ship and just being afloat! Afterwards, an exhibition of schools' follow-up work is held in the museum.

Some attempts have been made at inter-museum co-operation; for instance, working also with drama groups. In London in 1975 the Geffrye Museum, the National Army Museum and the National Portrait Gallery worked together on different aspects of the Civil Wars and brought in a travelling theatre group to dramatize incidents, make television programmes and help schools to recreate the period and its events.

Contents and Methods

The aims of museum education services are very flexible indeed; and deliberately so. In a profession which is still developing rapidly, where the museum has so much potential to offer, and where educational ideas and technology are constantly changing, educational activities within the museum must be ready to provide a great variety of methods through which people can receive insights into, and enjoyment of the collections.

Guided tours of the collections, except for small, specialized groups looking at small, specialized areas of the collections, are not generally encouraged; however, schools are gradually learning of the scope of museums to provide other approaches and facilities. It is interesting to note that at the time of writing more and more links are being formed between museums and historic houses; and between museums and ancient monument sites: in both, where there has been an absence of trained education staff, guided tours have often been the norm; it now seems likely that as a result of these contacts, such methods are more and more likely to disappear and be overtaken by more imaginative methods of involvement and enjoyment, both for adults and children. Museums with education services, and indeed often those who have none, usually have activities rooms and/or a lecture theatre with facilities both for children and for adults. The lecture theatre would normally be fitted out with a screen and audio-visual equipment. Particularly well equipped are the lecture theatres of the National Maritime Museum and of the Science Museum in London. A number of museums have built Children's Centres with self-contained units of activities rooms, cloakrooms, display areas and eating facilities. The Horniman Museum in London run by the Inner London Education Authority was the first to provide such a centre in 1969; in 1974, the National Maritime Museum opened the Half-Deck, with opportunities for informal practical work such as painting and modelling, a boat building workshop, and cloakroom and eating facilities in the mess deck.

Essential equipment for activities rooms would include; a large, flexible area to take comfortably the average-size school class - with washable floor surfaces and walls, stackable and washable-topped tables and chairs which may be arranged in many ways; audio-visual equipment such as might be provided for a lecture theatre, and a wide variety of electric points; painting, drawing and modelling materials, a large sink at a level suitable for use by children; display areas and/or cases. In addition, many such rooms have laboratory benches and laboratory facilities and equipment including gas taps; some have pottery kilns and wheels; at some also a library of reference books both for teachers and student teachers may include reference books, information sheets and reference material about the education service, the museum generally, and the local area, as well as examples of worksheets for use by school children in the museum.

Some museums provide other kinds of facilities and experiences, both for adults and for children. The Tate Gallery's education officer, for instance, has, during the past few years put on a number of exhibitions giving opportunities for self-guided exploration and experience, for example *Kidsplay I* and *Kidsplay II* and *Tate Games' 75*. A film was made of *Kidsplay* entitled *Beyond the Frame* and great interest was shown in a number of other countries, including Australia where the museum education officer accepted an invitation to give a lecture tour. The Victoria and Albert Museum put on an exhibition in 1975 called Body Box to explore the art of sculpture. A number of art galleries are well-known for giving opportunities for exploration through exhibition and experimental activity areas for both sculpture and painting, i.e. in Aberdeen, Sheffield, and Durham.

There is an increasing tendency too for museums to emphasize practical work and experiment and drama as a means of giving insights. The Geffrye Museum, through Molly Harrison's pioneering ideas and spirit, has long held a reputation for dramatic reconstruction of a period, using replica period costume so that children may, for instance, re-enact a scene in a period room of the museum. Such ideas are used in the Museum of Childhood at Sudbury Hall, Derbyshire, where Barbara Winstanley and John Hodgson have created displays with activities forming an integral part; for instance, a reconstructed chimney allows children to experience the terror of being climbing boys chimney-sweeping. Day visits to the house at Sudbury by schools might include such tasks, in appropriate costume, as scrubbing floors or laying fires. Clarke Hall Educational Museum near Wakefield, 1977 winner of the Pilgrim Trust Museum of the Year Award for the most outstanding small museum in the United Kingdom, is a 17th century yeoman farmer's house fully restored, refurnished and equipped with both original and replica equipment. This allows the practical use by children and teachers in period costume of the kitchen, the dairy and the weaving room, thereby integrating the practical and academic study of history, a learning technique appreciated by the modern archaeologist through reconstruction work. There are, too, a number of open-air museums where opportunities both for participation and for demonstration exist, for example Abbeydale Museum, Sheffield, Gladstone Pottery Museum, St. Fagan's, Ulster Folk and Transport Museum, the Weald and Downland, Ironbridge Gorge and Acton Scott Working Farm Museum.

Some museums are particularly well-known for their keeness to include fieldwork with museum visits, in order to extend appreciation and understanding of the museum's collections. At Bristol, for instance, street trails and town trails have been devised, sometimes in collaboration with the media as radio programmes for schools. Natural history and geology field work excursions are regularly undertaken in the local area. Often such fieldwork visits are carried out with schools (for instance, by the museum education officer for Devon, Leslie Jackman, who is also a well-known writer and broadcaster on natural history), very often, though, they are carried out with museum club activities for children at weekends and in holidays. The British Museum (Natural History), for instance, takes children on out-of-London fieldwork excursions. The Geffrye Museum in London, situated in the East End in a very definite and traditional east end community, takes children out to study their local environment; it also tries to involve the local community in its activities.

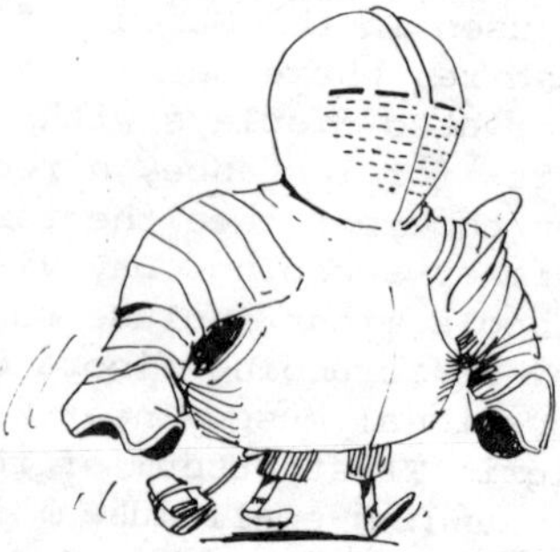

Many museums have a policy of going out to schools to keep in touch, to give talks, take teaching collections to handle in a classroom, observe the use of museum loan material and take part in follow-up activities. It is particularly valuable for schools in rural areas with high transport costs who are unable to get to their nearest museum or are in deprived areas of cities. However, a visit by a museum education officer is no substitute for a visit to the museum with its comprehensive collections.

For many years museum education services concentrated upon the developemnt of loan services. Indeed some services, particularly those run by Local Education Authorities and not based on a public museum, began by the provision of loan services only. Derbyshire, the Yorkshire Consortium and Nottinghamshire began this way, Derbyshire and Yorkshire later developed educational museums at Sudbury Hall and Clarke Hall respectively. A government report in 1963, known as the Rosse Report, made a particularly strong recommendation that the development of loan services, particularly in rural areas, should be encouraged. Such loan services include original material, models and sometimes replicas as well as original paintings, sculpture, drawings, prints, studio pottery, reproductions, films, slides, filmstrips, tape/slide programmes, photographs, gramophone records and cassettes covering not only music but also the spoken word, historical material, bird songs and sound effects.

Until comparatively recently museums were on the whole the only providers of the three dimensional audio-visual resources to schools; now, however, teachers' centres and resource units often provide audio-visual equipment and reprographic machinery as well as records, tapes, films, filmstrips and paper resource materials. This means that it is no longer so essential for museums to send out a loan case or kit including tapes, slides, film and documentary material together in one box with original material. Loan cases do still, however, very often contain this type of material in addition to museum specimens, models or replicas, together with notes for teachers, providing information and pointers to further useful book material or resources, relevant places to visit, etc., sometimes suggesting approaches to using the specimens or for follow-up work. Such loan collections in travelling cases, usually consisting of a small number of objects, for example objects from a Roman House: the 18th century tableware; Victorian lace; a blackbird; a working model of volcana, animal skulls'; or even a single object, are usually delivered (and collected) under the museum's administration to educational establishments within its Local Education Authority for periods of anything from a week to half-a-term, to a whole term; in some authorities, for example Bradford, teachers' centres are used for distributing under the administration of the museum, on a helpyourself basis. Travelling exhibitions are more generally used in polytechnics, colleges of further education, colleges of education, libraries, hospitals and other museums as a museum display to be visited; whereas museum schools' loan services provide loan cases for active use in the classroom itself, as an integrated part of classwork on a particular topic, at the request of a particular teacher, or group of teachers.

Experimental work has been carried out in neighbourhood museums in a number of areas, often on a temporary basis in connection with community festivals. Two particularly interesting developments have occurred quite recently in the use of mobile units: the Commonwealth Institute in London has a Commonwealth Caravan which is commissioned by museums and communities for exhibition in the provinces, demonstration of and participation in the cultural life of a particular Commonwealth country or countries. The aim behind this development is particularly to further understanding and appreciation of the life and culture of immigrant communities and to help to integrate immigrant and local populations. In Warwickshire, a mobile van exhibition unit has been set up, particularly to tour rural areas of the county with exhibitions of material from the county museum, to encourage investigation into the local environment by local communities, provide audio-visual or slide-tape programmes, and material of educational use to local schools. In Derbyshire an exhibition van will soon be specifically linking with groups of schools working on the county environmental studies project.

The museum attempts to provide facilities, displays and collections of objects, to be handled where possible for use both in the museum and in school, together with other audio-visual materials. Often it gives guidance both in preparation for work with such collections and for follow-up work.

Programmes - Activities Offered

Museum education services are dealing increasingly not only with schools, teachers and children, but also with adults - in fact, with every section of the public from 3 to 93! Schools generally are interested in all aspects of the museum's collections, particularly at the primary school stage and first and second years of secondary school, where many subjects are taught through topics rather than under academic subject headings. Since museums receive many more visits from primary schools than from secondary schools, there is much greater scope both for multidisciplinary subjects and for interdisciplinary approaches to the use of the collections, whereas at secondary school level a more conservative choice of topics prevails after the first two years, mainly because of the pressure towards public examination work.

Examples of interdisciplinary approaches may include geologist, naturalist, archaeologist and social historian specialists in a Schools Museum Service, integrating their approach to a local area to explain how it has developed through geological time onwards and how man has affected and changed the environment; such an approach gives a rounded understanding of an area. Or a topic such as wool might be treated from the historical, natural science, agricultural and craft points of view, including practical work in spinning, weaving and dyeing. The interdisciplinary possibilities of museum collections and the dependence of multidisciplinary expertise in the museum field opens up exciting and limitless possibilities for the museum educator faced with the very flexible syllabus found in schools in the United Kingdom.

Schools determine their own syllabuses. There has been an increasing tendency in recent years for schools to submit three examination syllabuses for the Certificate of Secondary Education for senior pupils to the Education Authorities. Museums are not only able to present wide-ranging teaching possibilities; in some cases, they have played an influential role in curriculum development schemes towards the making of such syllabuses. Nevertheless, there is no compulsion for any group or school class to visit any museum during their education.

How Are the Museum's Special Potentials as Education Instruments Used?

Museums may, of course, be used in hundreds of different ways with schools, and with children generally, sometimes fairly informally, sometimes with an academic approach, sometimes a practical - sometimes an imaginative and creative approach. It is generally felt that the importance of handling original material cannot be overestimated; but handling, of course, does not go far enough; demonstration - of how things work or how things are made - is very important indeed, but it is better still to be involved in the way something works, the way something is made, and practical participation is encouraged wherever possible.

Teaching collections are generally very much favoured among museum educationalists in this country and are used in the ways just mentioned; a questioning and self-discovering approach is encouraged, as is the use of the senses and extension into practical work including modelling, painting and drawing.

Such collections and activities may be employed together with audio-visual material; for example films, slides, filmstrips, overhead projector transparencies, tape recorders, record players, and sometimes even videotapes - though few museums have their own videotape equipment. These may be used in conjunction with the permanent galleries or with temporary exhibitions, possibly using worksheets as a method of directing attention to particular objects and particular questions, though such worksheets have to be constructed with care so as not to concentrate on the labels! Drawing as a method of encouraging close observation is still very much favoured as a means to this end.

Most school parties can only afford to come to the museum for one session, mainly because of transport costs; the visit might last for half a day, or sometimes a whole day. And within these constraints only a limited and short period type of practical work is possible. Saturday clubs and holiday activities and informal groups, however, have the chance to produce a sustained effort over a longer period of time, and might therefore work, for instance, on a videotape programme. Such activities as mounting exhibitions and collecting museum-type items to make a display are generally regarded as follow-up activities in school. With technical support and equipment from Bristol University, Bristol children one summer holiday learnt to use a portapak video machine: with this they made a programme based on a dramatic presentation by other children of Queen Elisabeth I's visit to Bristol in the 16th century, set in a 16th century room in a period house belonging to the museum. The programme included 16th century television commercials of, for example, the newly available potato, brought to this country at that time, the new addiction to pipe smoking with tobacco from the New World, where to buy the best ruffs, etc.

The Roles of Museum Staff and School Teachers in Educational Activities at Museums

There are some eighty-four full-time education services in museums in the United Kingdom. In these departments there may be more or less emphasis on schools as distinct from education as a whole; this depends very much on the policy and development of individual museums to what extent curatorial staff are involved in museum education work. It is noteworthy, however, that during recent years some museum education officers have become directors of museums and that there is a growing recognition of the importance in curatorial staff attitudes: increasingly the training of curatorial staff includes some awareness of their need to recognize the educational potential of the museum; it is hoped that this awareness will be very much extended to include some definite training as time goes on.

Local Education Authorities have a varied role to play in the planning and carrying through of museum education activities. In many instances they finance, or partly finance, a museum education service; sometimes indeed the museum itself may be administratively and financially linked with a Local Education Authority; but the chief day-to-day connection is with Local Education Authority personnel - advisers, support services, teachers' centres, field study centres*, and so on. Teachers may have strong or weak links with the museum, according to the type of service provided, the amount of in-service training, advice and information given, and whether teachers' workshop groups have been formed to involve themselves in the planning of work, be it in connection with new loan service, teaching kits, or whatever. Some teachers assist with less formal activities such as Saturday and holiday clubs, and a number of museums also employ student teachers in a voluntary capacity - for both experienced and student teachers this sort of experience is valuable; many museum education services have a definite policy of advising and providing information so that teachers can use the museum's resources for their classes. Although there is no compulsion to bring classes to the museum, the large

---

* *Field Study Centres:* nationally, locally or independently organized centres which may or may not be residential, where school pupils and/or students may go for a course of anything from a day to a week, or perhaps even longer. Usually the purpose is local studies - natural history, archaeology, local history, geology, including the use of local trails; or outdoor pursuits such as rock-climbing, sailing, canoeing, caving, waling, camping etc. These two types of activity may also be combined. Usually the centre is based in a particular type of environment eg. by the coast, on an island, in a forest, in a mountainous area etc.

number makes it impossible and uneconomic for the museum staff to deal with every group. There are, of course, advantages in using their expertise; but there are also advantages in a class teacher, with some training and assistance, using the museum's resources for him/herself. In planning activities, school pupils themselves are not consulted generally: however, the teaching system is so flexible in primary schools that if a class becomes deeply involved and interested in a particular topic related to the museum and its collections, the museum can usually accommodate and extend those interests.

Many museum education services have advisory committees comprising representatives of various levels of teaching and related services, for example, university and college of education lecturers, Teachers' Centre wardens, primary and secondary school teachers, a special schools (handicapped) representative, an LEA representative, etc.

It is also common practice for museum education officers to take part in the training of as many student teachers in their area as possible. For the student who can be made aware, through a course or series of courses, of the potential of the museum is much more likely to be able to assimilate and use museum education services than the busy, harassed, practising teacher who hears about museums later on in his career. Such training may take the form of lectures, practical workshop groups, teaching practice in the museum or the occasional slotting in of a student or group of students to an education project taking place in the museum. Opportunities are given for looking behind the scenes as well, very often - for instance, in stores and workshops.

Practical aspects of bringing a class on a visit may be combined with work on particular academic disciplines, topics or approaches to topics. Information sheets, handouts and examples of worksheets will generally be available at such courses. Tapes, films and slides may also be used.

The two forms of training for museum staff increasingly include education training for curatorial staff: full-time postgraduate courses in museum studies at Leicester University, and in Art Gallery subjects at Manchester University; and the part-time method favoured by most museum staff, of the Museums Association Diploma, comprising three ten-day residential courses, a minimum of eight essays for and three visits to a tutor, and the passing of written and practical examinations. Museum education studies, like other curatorial disciplines, are the subject of one of the three residential courses and of special papers or questions in the examination papers.

As far as other seminars and group training facilities are concerned, the Group for Educational Services in Museums as the national body on the subject is the main organizer, sometimes in conjunction with other bodies such as the Museums Association or Area Museum Councils, sometimes with local museums themselves. Since 1974 regional branches of the Group have developed in different parts of the country, and their meetings often contain a training element in the way of discussing problems and topics of current interest - often bringing in people from other walks of educational life.

Most museum education staff members come into museums after successful teaching experience; a degree with a teaching qualification is normally held or a College of Education teacher training: the former is normally preferred. It is strongly felt that, in services where such a large amount of work is done with schools, understanding and experience of the school curriculum, teaching and practical problems and school opportunities are necessary, educational experience, together with a relevant academic qualification or interest, is generally considered desirable for entry into museum education work.

The residential course of the Museums Association Diploma in Educational Studies covers as many aspects as possible of museum education work through lectures, observation, practical and workshop sessions, visits to museums and educational and other relevant establishments.

It is not easy to give an appraisal of the use of educational resources of museums by the national education system, since that system allows so much freedom and flexibility; however, it may generally be said that schools, colleges and universities increasingly use their services; also that the use of the museum by infant and nursery schools - i.e. for use by the lowest age group - is increasing. The wider possibilities of what a museum has to offer in terms of educational potential are being more and more appreciated by more and more sections of education and of the public.

While not necessarily or specifically mentioned in school curricula, a large percentage of schools goes to museums regularly, specifically to study certain aspects, for example life in Prehistoric Times, Dinosaurs, British Birds, etc. An increasing number of textbooks of the newer topic book, work card or teaching/ learning pack variety also encourages schools to use museums in connection with various topics or in connection with fieldwork.

An investigation is currently taking place on the use made of museums and museum education departments in teacher training. The ICOM CECA working party on training has this subject under review in this country.

Information

On a national scale, information about museum education activities is available both from the Museums Association and more particularly from GESM with whom they work closely. This latter body has some 250 members; institutional members include museums and museum education services teachers' centres, and colleges of education, individual membership includes members of the teaching profession and also model makers, who are encouraged to join. The aims of the Group are to promote and coordinate interest in and information about, educational work in museums and art galleries, by pooling and exchanging ideas and information concerning the work already being done in and by museums in this country and abroad, and by extending among educationalists and teachers an appreciation of how museums can help them and their students.

The officers of GESM deal with many and varied enquiries concerning museum education activities and careers in museum education. They have been responsible for a number of publications, which include a handlist of museum education services with summaries of their main activities. GESM publishes a quarterly newsletter; its other activities include regional meetings, occasional seminars, and an annual conference; its Committee is also the British National Committee for ICOM CECA.

While there are broad common bases to all museum education programmes, individual museum education services also produce their own publicity and information. These might include teaching packs; information sheets about the service, the museum's collections and the local area; worksheets for use in museum galleries, slide packs, and tapes. The Area Museum Council for the Midlands Education panel has also produced a map and information about museum education services* in the region. Loan services invariably publish catalogues of their collections which are issued to the schools and colleges they serve.

There are a number of channels for communication with schools and other educational organizations and these vary from place to place; however, a typical example might be that of Bristol, where the Local Education Authority's weekly mailing to schools is also used by the Museum Education Service, (independent schools have to be circulated separately). Circulars of the term teaching programme and loan service are circulated in this way as are programmes of in-service training to teachers. A curriculum bulletin is produced by the LEA which goes out to schools approximately once a month, and this may be used for current news or to emphasize further information already distributed. An in-service training brochure goes out to all schools from the local authority and this repeats once more information about courses at the museum. Many museum education services address their programmes etc. specifically to the staff

---

* *Area Museum Services:* regional organizations covering the different areas of the British Isles to provide display, conservation, education and training services to the museums in their area, and particularly to the smaller museums. Some museums have museum educational panels, with representatives from museum education services in their area. Regional sub-groups of the Group for Educational Services in Museums also liaise closely with them where possible.

noticeboard in a school, since otherwise they may never get further than the head's office! However, some museum education services have successfully encouraged schools to appoint museum education representatives to act in liaison with the museum. It is also found useful to have a distinctive housestyle and colour for museum education publications so that there is a regularly recognizable communication for staff to pick out. Some museums use the Local Education Authority mailing list exclusively; many use their own mailing channel. Teachers' centres, Field Study Centres and Colleges of Education might also make information available to teachers and student teachers in their area.

In addition, museums often hold open days, half-days or evenings for teachers, groups of teachers, or local teaching societies, either on specific topics or in order to talk generally about facilities. Such meetings might include a tour of loan service stores and workshops, tours of galleries, displays of work done in the museum, displays of recent additions to the loan collections.

Problems and Future Plans

Many of the current problems are similar to those of other countries. However, some may be peculiar to the United Kingdom; there is, of course, great variation in the problems facing different museums even in one country. Some Museums, for instance, may have old displays which are difficult to use, both from the point of view of the display itself, and from the point of view of spacing in galleries to allow adequate access. However, such problems are being resolved more and more through the very willing co-operation of curatorial staff and of designers. Curatorial attitudes some years ago of suspicion towards museum education services have now generally been replaced by positive co-operation and the common viewpoint of the museum as provider of a public service. This has in turn meant that where possible teaching and lecture room space and equipment are recognized as essential requirements, although in practical terms not always possible.

Most authorities see an education service both as a necessary and a prestige service. Schools, and other educational institutions too, increasingly use such services and are in general better oriented towards

good use of the museum than some years ago. Some however, unfortunately still regard a visit to a museum as an afternoon out rather than an integrated part of work done in school; some still try to fit in too many activities in one day, visiting not only the museum but a number of other places too, thereby providing a mentally and physically overloaded day for their pupils. There is still room for a tremendously increased amount of in-service training of teachers and student teachers both in regard to the provincial and particularly the national museums which draw on a very widely scattered visiting school public. Communications with schools also remains a very widespread problem since so much paper never reaches the teaching staff in general, particularly in large comprehensive schools.

However, increased use of museum education services by schools and teachers, both for teaching, loan and information/advisory services, means that demands on museum education staff time are too high. In the current financial situation though, much use is being made of the Job Creation Scheme whereby unemployed people, particularly unemployed teachers, may be taken on by a service for a period of time to work on special projects which could not otherwise be carried out; of course such schemes require careful training and supervision, but are generally found to be extremely useful both to the museum and to the people so temporarily employed.

Finances are always in need of improvement, both for extension of services and in terms of staff salaries. There is also some variation in terms of employment and salary scale; museum education officers may be paid on curatorial salary rates with the same amount of leave, or on LEA advisers' salary rates or on teachers' salary rates, again with appropriate amounts of leave. Teachers' and advisers' salaries and leave allowances tend to be much more generous than curatorial rates of pay and holidays; and yet if a museum education officer receives higher pay than his museum director, difficulties may understandably arise. It is hoped that in future more standardized conditions of pay and leave prevail, tied in to educational and museum professional qualifications.

It is also hoped that, with more active participation than ever before in international meetings, more money might be made available in future not only to attend conferences abroad but also to take part in further exchanges, both of groups and of individuals. Such participation would not only broaden the outlook of the profession, but also provide a better balance between work with schools and work with the public in general.

Further, the museum education movement in this country is spreading gradually more evenly through England, Scotland, Wales and Northern Ireland, but is by no means a complete network yet. The Group for Educational Services in Museums hopes to encourage the further spread of such services and has on its executive committee representatives of the interests of all four areas of the United Kingdom. Since 1975 it has also encouraged regional activities by its members and these sub-groups are now thriving.

Methods of communication with schools in terms of teaching and access to museum collections have recently been more of a problem than previously because of transport costs involved in bringing children to the museum. Loan services are, as ever, most valuable; portable exhibitions are sometimes available too, either for individual schools or for a group of schools to use; and museum education officers recognize the need for flexibility of method - frequently going out to schools taking teaching collections with them; or advising on the use of loan collections in schools. However, while transport costs are a definite problem to schools - particularly in deprived areas - it is generally found that if museums can provide good enough resources, schools will find the wherewithal to come. It is the enthusiasm for the educational experience which provides the impetus.

United States of America

Bonnie Pitman-Gelles

Museums are vibrant institutions, housing the wonders of the natural and man-made world and reflecting the creativity of artists, scientists, craftsmen, and writers. They are, first of all, collections of objects and specimens: butterflies, lace, dinosaur bones, Indian pottery, suits of armor, Western paintings, wooden houses, light sculptures, documents, Greek sculpture, reptiles -- the list is endless. People come individually and collectively in family and school groups to see these collections. Whatever their motivation, they come primarily to look, to study, and often to participate.

The basic function of a museum is to collect and preserve these objects and specimens and to display them on some regular basis to the public. Museums also provide innovative programmes and exhibitions, unique contributions to the cultural life of a community. Further, a museum acts as a catalyst, introducing people to new ideas and areas of interest and motivating them to seek further knowledge through study and return visits. Through their educational programmes, museums help participants develop their perceptual skills so that they can learn how to look and discover new relationships on their own. Exhibits not only provide an opportunity for visitors to look but to think, to explore, to wonder, and to investigate.

Today museum buildings include not only exhibition halls, auditoriums, classrooms, and libraries but also scientific laboratories, participatory galleries, art studios, gardens, nature trails, research centres, planetariums, aquariums, insect zoos, and media production facilities.

Museums are open to the public. People may browse, ask questions, study, and often even borrow or rent such things as paintings, fossils, live animals, and exhibit cases to take home or to the classroom. Their reasons for coming are diverse: to observe the curiosities in a turn-of-the-century blacksmith shop, to examine the infinite variety of colour in butterfly wings, to observe the habitat of the mountain lion.

No longer are museums simply cabinets of curiosities, rather, they have become places providing unique educational resources and opportunities. They are environments, where one can study the entire animal kingdom, objects from ancient civilizations, rocks, and fossils or grow a garden, paint, write poetry, or operate a computer. According to Alma Wittlin, children's museums 'have a niche among the pioneers of contemporary education. For decades they have been appealing to the child's otherwise neglected tactile sense in exploring his environment'.(132, p. 235)

A variety of programmes are offered both inside and outside of museums. Those developed for use inside the museum help to draw the visitor into learning experiences that utilize some of the special resources of the collections. Tours, workshops, clubs, classes, demonstrations, and festivals are all a part of this type of programming. Special programmes are also widely available for the partially sighted, blind, deaf, retarded and physically handicapped.

A brief review of some of the types of programmes offered by museums follows.

Special Education Galleries, Discovery Rooms. Exhibits focus on objects, concepts, and themes. Reinforced by an array of sensory and participatory techniques, they can actively involve the visitor in the learning experience. With the further aid of lables and written supplemental material, exhibits can stimulate the imagination of visitors and help them establish a frame of reference for future visits. Interactive exhibits provide direct experiences with real materials.

Exhibits that involve the public in the learning process through participation have been widely used by science-technology centres and children's museums across the country.

The Exploratorium identifies itself as a perceptual science museum that invites visitors to learn through participation and exploration. Like many other science-technology centres, it is barrier-free. The director, Frank Oppenheimer, has conceived the exhibits as props in a 'pedagogical chain'. The Exploratorium has multiple and contextually different examples of the same concept. This type of exhibit presentation allows visitors to learn for themselves and not from a single example of each effort or process. Exhibits survey the world of light and colour, waves, the role of the brain in creating a sense of depth, eye logic, technology of lasers and television. 'Explainers' are always in public areas repairing exhibits, answering questions, and demonstrating principles. The Exploratorium is a library of props that allow the visitor to gain first-hand contact with natural phenomena. An example is the Enchanted Tree which responds to singing, clapping, or talking as the coloured lights move up and down responding to sound. It is both a sculpture and an exhibit on computer technology.

The Object Gallery of the Florida State Museum in Gainsville is designed to complement the major exhibits programme of the museum. The purpose of this room is to help the visitor better understand the collections and their value as teaching and research tools. The gallery contains some traditional exhibit cases, as well as vertical files with exhibits on how to identify birds, snakes, and other specimens; study areas with tables and chairs; aquariums and terrariums; and over 200 drawers of objects (i.e., projectile points, kachina dolls, pine cones, landsnails).

The American Museum of Natural History in New York City has a number of different educational spaces specifically designed to involve the visitor and to complement the exhibits. It has the *Alexander M. White Natural Science Center,* a teaching/exhibit space that describes the nature of New York City for the young people. The exhibit, a total of thirteen compact units, begins with concrete and asphalt -- the ground city youngsters walk on -- and moves to other familiar street scenes, such as sidewalk excavation exposing utility pipes and cables, a tree on the street, a vacant lot, a store window. In each unit, a built-in activity enables the visitor to participate rather than to view passively. A staff member is always on hand to answer questions.

The People Center, another interpretative facility at the American Museum of Natural History, gives visitors intimate contact with performers or teachers and serves as a teaching space, demonstration centre, and performance area. Exhibits, stage areas, and informal seating arrangements allow visitors to observe and participate in learning about other cultures and the values of different societies. Exhibits and activities in the People Centre juxtapose contemporary Western forms with those from other times and places. Music or dance from New York City and Thailand may occur simultaneously; chamber music may alternate with Ghanaian drumming. A Monopoly set or a contemporary American ceramic piece may be placed with games and pottery from other cultures to point up cultural similarities as well as differences.

The Children's Museum of Boston takes this emphasis on understanding the child's relationship to the natural world one step further. *The Visitor Center* is a learning environment where children interact with museum objects. In Grandmother's Attic, for example, children are free to discover something about domestic life at the turn of the century. They may dress up in antique clothing, play school at the old desks, churn butter, braid rugs, or crank up a phonograph and hear a tune. In the Japanese home, children try on clothing, make and eat Japanese food, and sing folk songs in the two-room house. The activities and exhibits are designed to develop the children's understanding of the similarities and differences in American and Japanese cultures. Most of the learning spaces are staffed continually so that visitors can be encouraged to interact with the objects and can have their questions answered.

In its new quarters, the Brooklyn Children's Museum incorporates its architecture, its collections, permanent exhibit structures, retail shop, workshop programmes, children's library, and take-home collection into a single system of interactive elements. This system constitutes a participatory learning environment in which children may seek an understanding of themselves and the world in which they live.

The museum's innovative architecture turns the building itself into an exhibit. Construction materials and methods are exposed throughout; colour-coded pipes and ventilation ducts, laminated wooden beams, bare concrete walls, nuts and bolts, hollow-tile or concrete blocks turned right-side-out on one wall and wrong-side-out on another. Perhaps even more striking is the use of familiar large-scale objects from urban and rural settings as built-in components of the museum: a 1907 trolley car kiosk as the main entrance; an oil storage tank as an enclosed indoor auditorium; super highway signs as museum signs on the roof; steel l-beams as benches; a corrugated steel drainage culvert as a 'People Tube' corridor; park benches, pathways, and lamposts as part of the earth-covered roof; and a blue porcelainized grain silo as a rooftop fire escape.

The main exhibition area of the museum consists of four giant steps of levels, terraced downward form the corner entrance of the boxshaped, semi-underground building. The corrugated steel 'People Tube' forms a ramp extending from the main entrance diagonally across all four levels and providing ready access for handicapped visitors. The visitor finds the bulk of the museum's exhibits in this main area. Here are the large-scale permanently installed and visitor-operated technological artifact -- a stream of water with locks, dams, waterfalls, and waterwheels; a steam engine; a windmill driven by giant fans; a greenhouse; a ripple tank. Interspersed with these large technological exhibits are artifacts from the museum's collections.

Orientation Theatres and Galleries. These media presentations introduce the visitor to the exhibits and provide additional material on the collections or artists. Such programmes are used in the Virginia Museum of Art, Philadelphia Museum of Art, the Peninsula Nature Science Center, Virginia, and at various historic and national parks.

Self-Guided Tours. Many museums (e.g., the Metropolitan Museum of Art, the Field Museum, Florida State Museum) have designed materials to be used by students and teachers during their tour of the collections. These materials include treasure hunts and thematic tours. Audio-tape tours such as those at the Milwaukee Art Center and the Boston Science Museum are also used by a number of museums to help direct the visitor through the galleries.

Demonstrations. Science museums have been effectively using participatory demonstrations of basic scientific principles in exhibit areas for many years. The Chicago Museum of Science and Industry and the Museum of Science in Boston provide demonstrations of magnetism, electricity, optics, sound and other related subjects. At the Children's Museum of Indianapolis and at Old Economy Village in Ambridge, Pennsylvania, spinning and carding demonstrations are given by costumed interpreters illustrating the lives of the early settlers in the community. Most of the living historical villages and farms have costumed interpreters who role-play the daily life activities of the people who lived on that farm or in the town. They help the visitors to understand the ways people lived: the functional use of tools, methods of cooking, planting crops, raising a family, purchasing goods, going to church.

Tours. Gallery talks are still the most widely used programme format, though the techniques of presentation and level of student involvement have changed dramatically. Many tours are structured around a theme (e.g., Family Life, Adaptation and Evolution, The Culture of China). The museum staff usually determines two or three main concepts that can be illustrated through the presentation of a few artifacts. If possible, students should be allowed to handle objects (e.g., hooves, jaws, brushes and palettes of the artist, pioneer tools, and utensils). In other instances, children participate in activities, such as churning butter, experimenting with electricity, writing a poem, or doing creative movement in the galleries. Teaching techniques range from asking questions to dressing in costumes or engaging in perception games in the galleries. The length and scope of a tour can vary from twenty minutes to a series of six visits. Some museums also are collaborating with each other in the development of programmes. The tours are conducted by a member of the staff or a volunteer docent.

Single Visits. Teachers bring their classes to the

museum for an introduction in the form of a general or thematic tour of the collections. Many museums have expanded this experience to include handling objects or participating in short term activities such as cooking a meal, carding and spinning wool, or handling small objects in the galleries such as bones, fur, clothing or tools which help to heighten their awareness of the objects behind the glass cases.

Series Visits. Usually focused on a theme and frequently tied to the school curriculum, such visits allow for concentrated study of the collections. Often the teacher workbooks and workshops are developed to accompany these programmes. Colonial Williamsburg and the Brooklyn Museum of Art are among the many museums that offer this type of programming for children and teachers.

Museums and schools. Traditionally, museums have established close relationships with local school systems. In fact, some youth museums were founded by teachers interested in providing additional educational opportunities to students (e.g., The Children's Museum of Boston, the Fort Worth Museum of Science and History, the Jacksonville (Florida) Children's Museum, and the Fernbank Science Center). Founded by the DeKalb Board of Education in Atlanta, the Fernbank Science Center still is an integral part of the school system, with exhibits and after school programmes in the physical and life sciences and natural history.

Some school districts assign teachers to the museum. The Charlotte Nature Museum in North Carolina, the Fernbank Science Center, and the Philadelphia Museum of Art all have this type of arrangement. Such an allocation is sometimes easier for the school district to make because today there are often more tenured teachers than money to be distributed. There are advantages and disadvantages to having a teacher from the school system assigned to work at the museum. On the positive side, the teacher or co-ordinator can bring to the museum a knowledge of the curriculum and resource materials currently being used by the system; further, they usually know the types of programmes that appeal to both teachers and children. Knowledge of the school system, its schedules and regulations, is also an advantage when developing new programmes.

Some school districts pay museums a set amount for each child who attends the museum for a specific programme. This fee reimburses the museum for its educational services -- professional time, materials, and facilities. Another approach to school museum co-operation has been developed as a result of jointly funded federal programmes that may include curriculum development projects such as those at the Minneapolis Institute of Arts and the Missouri Botanical Gardens. These programmes are mutually beneficial to the museum and the school system, since they require, among other things, teacher training and in-depth programming for the children at the museum.

Many museums have *integrated their programmes into the curriculum of the local schools*. This arrangement requires that all children at a specified grade level come to the museum for a programme such as space science, art history, health education or American history. These programmes are carefully designed to complement the students' work in schools and serve to enrich their understanding of a culture, country or scientific concept. The programmes can be a requirement of the students' studies such as those at the Fernbank Science Center in Atlanta and the New Orleans Museum of Art, or they can be a voluntary selection for a field trip as demonstrated by the St. Petersburgh Art Museum in Florida and the Boston Museum of Fine Arts.

Museums also are used as *extensions of the schools'* resources providing indepth series of classes for students in the museum for which they receive credit. Examples of this type of programme are the School in the Exploratorium, the Search Program at the Indianapolis Museum of Art and the Cleveland Health Museum - students and teachers attend the museum for a specified period of time and use the collections and resources as a primary focus of their educational programmes. The Boston Zoological Society has developed a bilingual wildlife education programme which helps children to learn about animals and other cultures, and at the same time develop their reading and math skills.

Advanced Placement Programmes, Independent Research Projects and Internships for Credit are another effective way museums and schools are working together. In these programmes individual students work with the museum's staff, usually on a specified project for which they receive credit hours. Programmes such as these are found around the country including the Pacific Science Center, Cleveland Museum of Art and the Boston Children's Museum.

Curriculum Development programmes which bring together

museums and schools to design and develop curriculum materials are increasing as a result of increased federal support. The Minneapolis Institute of Art has received a grant to design an elementary level curriculum that will explore concepts in the humanities such as truth, justice, love and beauty as seen in works of art in different cultures and periods of history. At the Lawrence Hall of Science in California curricula are being developed in computer education for deaf students, astronomy for elementary grades, and science enrichment activities for the visually handicapped. The Roger Williams Zoo Park in Providence, Rhode Island, in collaboration with the public schools developed an education programme for grades five and six which supplements the science curriculum and utilizes the Zoo as an educational resource.

Collaborative Projects, such as those in Cleveland, Ohio, and Oakland, California, are designed to interrelate the resources of the entire community. Focussing on a theme, such as African art or the history of the court system, participants visit the zoo, court house, historical society, art museum, and other institutions in the course of their study.

Teacher Workshops. Museum educators have become increasingly aware of the need to help teachers and parents understand ways to utilize the resources of the museum. Workshops can serve many purposes: an orientation to the collections, a forum for ideas, a laboratory for learning new skills, new ways of teaching and involving children, a session on how to take classes through the museum without the assistance of the museum staff. The formats and topics vary widely and depend on the particular goals of the programme and the restrictions on the teachers time. In some communities museums are working with

local colleges to provide college credit for the training teachers receive at the museum. The Lawrence Hall of Science in California and Old Sturbridge Village in Massachussetts offer extensive teacher-training programmes which are designed to help teachers learn how to integrate the museums resources into their daily curricula. Such workshops are becoming standard programmes for many museums.

Junior Curators, Interns, Guides, Explainers, Student Advisory Boards. Young people in many museums help to design exhibits, conduct research, collect specimens, develop programmes, guide visitors, maintain exhibits and give demonstrations in science and history areas. For example, at the Stanford Museum and Nature Center in Connecticut, students assist with the animals in the farm, zoo and Discovery Room.

Research Programmes. Advanced students in specialized fields of study work with museum collections, equipment, and professionals. The Oregon Museum of Science and Industry in Portland, the Maryland Science Center in Baltimore, and the Florida State Museum in Gainesville provide such indepth research experiences. The Hagley Museum in Wilmington, Delaware, holds an advance research project for senior Girl Scouts, who use the collections to develop teaching programmes for the younger scouts.

Classes and Workshops. Archaeology, entomology, mammalogy, mineralogy, ornithology, paleontology, dance, mime, printmaking, weaving, film making, painting, quilting, puppeteering, and cooking are but a few of the courses offered in museum schools after school and on week-ends. The Fort Worth Museum of Science and History offers natural science and history-oriented classes for pre-schoolers, as well as wide range of classes for children six to sixteen. Parent-child workshops are a regular feature of many museums, including the Metropolitan Museum of Art and the Indianapolis Children's Museum.

Summer Workshops, Classes, Festivals. With more time available, the summer is a particularly active programme period for museums. New York's Staten Island Children's Museum has developed a programme on sculpture and the environment. The New York Botanical Garden offers children an opportunity to grow, tend, and harvest vegetables from their own garden plot. Old Sturbridge Village has a week-long day programme for youngsters, who dress in costume and work as apprentices in the Village. The New Orleans Museum of Art co-ordinates one of their summer programmes with summer day camps to provide museum experiences for the handicapped and training for camp counselors. The Oregon Museum of Science and Industry has several campsites that involve children in collecting marine and fossil specimens and carrying on experiments in the marine biology laboratory.

Residencies. Artists-in-residence at museums include a printmaker at the National Collection of Fine Arts, Washington, D.C., and a poet at the Jacksonville Children's Museum, Florida.

Festivals and Events. Pet and science fairs are standard special events at many youth museums. The New Muse in New York holds an old fashioned street fair each summer with exhibits, entertainment, and delicacies for sale. The Cloisters in another section of New York provides a medieval festival complete with a market place, banners, and music. The Baltimore Museum of Art has special family days focusing on participatory art activities that often relate to special exhibits.

Auditorium, Theatre. Puppet presentations, stage plays, films, and dance performances are regular features at museums with such a facility. New York City's Jewish Museum and the Kansas Museum of Natural History in Lawrence also use their facilities for storytelling sessions.

Libraries. Many museums, such as the Brooklyn Children's Museum, have special libraries that loan books and artifacts to children.

Resource Centres, Recycle Centres. The Children's Museum in Boston sells recycled industrial by-products and furnishes ideas for recycling and using the results in the classroom. GAME* in New York is a resource centre for art and museum experiences related to the school curriculum. The St. Louis Museum of Art has an extensive Teacher Resource Center. The Milwaukee Public Museum and the Museum of Science, St. Paul, have trading posts that provide children with a chance to trade their shells, fossils, and insects to help develop and improve their own collections.

Due to distances and other factors, not all children can visit a museum regularly. Therefore, numerous programmes, exhibits, and materials have been designed to bring the museum to children in schools or community centres or on television. Some examples follow.

---

* Growth through Art and Museum Experience

Resource Packages. Slides and reproduced documents are designed to introduce the museum's collections and to supplement the language, social studies, and humanities programmes in the school. The National Archives, National Gallery of Art, and Detroit Institute of Arts are among the many museums distributing this type of material which can effectively be used in preparation or as a follow-up for the museum visit.

Loan Exhibits and Materials. Boxes, trunks, suitcases, and portable exhibits bring artifacts and specimens into the school classroom. Such items as turtles, rabbits, dioramas, ceramic materials, and African and Indian masks are available for loan from museums, accompanied by films, teacher manuals, and suggested activities. Many museums have developed such resource units (i.e., the Valentine Museum in Richmond, Virginia, the Colorado Historical Society in Denver and the Milwaukee Public Museum).

Classroom Presentations. Artifacts, art works, and live animals are taken into classrooms by the staff and volunteers in many museums. Presentations vary in length from twenty minutes to two hours. In general, the classrooms are located within an hours' driving distance from the museum. Activities range from presentations by costumed interpreters to travelling science programmes sent from the Maryland Science Center in Baltimore. The Sunrise Museum in Charlston, West Virginia, and the Staten Island Zoo in New York have developed programmes using live animals in the classroom.

Field Trips and Excursions. Archaeological digs and trips to historic and ecological sites integrate the study of the collections with new surroundings. Such programmes are provided by historical and anthropological museums, nature centres, and science-technology centres (i.e., Memphis Pink Palace, Oregon Museum of Science and History, Corpus Christi Museum).

Walking Tours. Strolls through the city to study the environment and architecture have been developed by historic, natural history, and art museums in such cities as New York, Chicago, and San Francisco.

Publications. The Smithsonian Institution has initiated a new publication called *Art to Zoo*, which offers the classroom teacher ideas for using the museums, zoos, parks, and libraries in their community. *Art Resource* packages of the Indianapolis Museum of Art provide teachers with ideas on how to integrate the resources of their community into their programmes. *Ancient News,* a newspaper put out by children, is distributed by the Elvehjem Art Center at the University of Wisconsin in Madison. *Roots,* a publication of the Minnesota Historical Society in St. Paul, is available to teachers and students. Workbooks for teachers and students have been produced by a number of museums, including the New York Historical Society in Cooperstown and the New Orleans Museum of Art.

Museums on Wheels, Art Crafts, Art Buses, Vans, Mobile Trucks. These programmes bring collections and experiences in the arts, science, and history to people who may not be able to come to the museums. Ringling Museum of Art in Sarasota, Florida, the Hudson River Museum in Yonkers, New York, the Museum of New Mexico in Santa Fe, and the Virginia Museum of Fine Arts in Richmond take art works and artists to schools in the community in various kinds of mobile units. Lawrence Hall of Science in Berkeley, California, has a van that serves as a resource for science and mathematics teachers. The Boston Museum of Transportation has a troupe of professional actors who perform at auditoriums and community centres.

Media. After designing Do-ITs, simple scientific experiments using materials found in the home to make colour wheels and slide rules, Philadelphia's Franklin Institute placed instructions for the experiments on Tasty Cake packages for regional distribution. Regular television shows are given by the director and staff of the the Corpus Christi Museum and the Fort Worth Museum of Science and History. The Alaska State Museum in Juneau develops educational programmes for state wide distribution on the educational television network.

This chapter focuses on the development of youth education programmes in the United States. It does not attempt to present a comprehensive survey of the educational activities in this country but rather focuses the readers' attention on the range of interesting programmes available to children, teachers, and parents.

Museum education has rapidly developed since World War II as a result of increased public interest and support. Despite the diversity in museums type, size, governing authority, and location, a survey conducted in

1973 and published in *Museums USA*, showed a general agreement among museum directors that education of the public was an important responsibility of the institution. This emphasis on education is reflected in the types of programmes conducted, because in addition to the recognized importance of the exhibition as an educational resource, many of the museums surveyed scheduled some types of educational activities directed towards a specific audience.

In the past few years a number of important publications on museum education has been produced. These have included surveys of the educational resources and programmes in museums throughout an entire region of the country or the documentation of the extensive programmes available in New York City. In addition, two new books have carefully reviewed the developments of educational programmes and methods of interpretation in history and art museums.

Newsletters, surveys and other forms of communication are being developed so that museum educators can share their successes and failures, methods of evaluation and programme development with each other. (2,87)

The future of museums in the United States is both complex and exciting. Increased demands by the public for use of the museum have expanded the types of exhibitions and programmes that are available. The shortages of fuel during the recent winters have required reduced operations by some museums located in the northern regions of the country. Increased costs for 'gas' have sometimes curtailed the numbers of school visits. Increased costs to operate the museum, to provide proper climate conditions for the collections, and guards, have resulted in a reduction in the hours that the museum is open to the public.

However, many museums are learning to overcome these restrictions. Programmes on energy conservation are being offered throughout the country. New surveillance equipment is being designed and installed to reduce the number of guards needed in the galleries. The use of television as a part of the programmes offered by museums has been expanding and is rapidly becoming an effective educational tool. People have recognized the valuable role that museums play in their lives.

Federal and private support has been increasing as demonstrated by the many museums that are moving into new buildings, refurbishing existing structures and expanding their facilities. The establishment of the Institute for Museum Services in the United States Office of Education is an important step for all museums as this new agency of the government will provide support for the operating costs of these cultural resources.

Museums are beginning to deal with a much broader audience. No longer are school children and patrons the primary visitors. Handicapped, elderly and adult visitors regularly come to the museum or the museum brings its programmes and collections to them. The role of the museum within the community is expaniing as the public begins to understand how to look at the collections and the museum learns how to design programmes that are relevant to many different people. As a result of the expanded use of the museums, it is becoming a resource for learning throughout people's lives, much like libraries. Collaboration between the universities, community centres, and other cultural institutions has increased as museums share their experiences and diversify their programmes to meet the ever-increasing demands.

In 1976, a Center for Museum Education was established at George Washington University in Washington, D.C. This resource centre has files that cover a wide range of topics, audience interest, programme and exhibition formats and training projects with information from all types of museums throughout the country. The centre publishes indexes of its holdings four times a year and has developed a number of resource information packages on topics of interest such as evaluation, lifelong lear-learning and docent training. The staff of the centre will also research individual requests for information at a small fee.

In 1973 the Standing Professional Committee on Museum Education was formed under the auspices of the American Association of Museums.

This article has been adapted from a forthcoming book by Bonnie Pitman-Gelles, edited by Aubyn Kendall, Fort Worth Museum of Science and History, Texas. The manuscript research was completed with a grant from the National Museum Act, Administered by the Smithsonian Institution to the American Association of Youth Museums.

List of contributors

Airey, Victoria, Schools Service Organizer, City of Bristol Art Gallery and Museum, United Kingdom.

Aît-Djafer, M'Hamed, Director of the Ecole de plein air et de perfectionnement, Ben-Rouilah, El-Biar, Algiers, Algeria.

Arinze, Emmanuel, Museum Education Officer, National Museum, Lagos, Nigeria.

Campos, Carmo Cabral, Education Service, Museu Nacional de Soares dos Reis, Oporto, Portugal.

Chongkol, Chira, Director, National Museum, Bangkok, Thailand.

Destrée-Heymans, Thérèse, Education Service, Dynamusee Royal Museums of Art and History, Brussels, Belgium.

Debrovolskaya, V., Head of Department at the State Russian Museum, U.S.S.R.

Gee, Maureen, Education Officer, British Columbia Provincial Museum, Victoria, Canada.

Kahler, Manfred, Studienrat, Weimar, German Democratic Republic.

Kureeva, I., Head of Department at the State Hermitage Museum, U.S.S.R.

Konaré, A. Oumar, Ministry of Arts and Culture, Bamako, Mali.

Novogilova, L., Director of the State Russian Museum, U.S.S.R.

Nteta, Doreen, Curator of Education, National Museum and Art Gallery, Gaborone, Botswana.

Olofsson, Ulla Keding, Head of Planning, Riksutställningar, formely Secretary General of CECA, Sweden.

Peltier, Rodolfo, Director, National Museum of Pedagogics, Mexico City, Mexico.

Pitman-Gelles, Bonnie, Chairperson, American Association of Museums, Committee on Museums Education, United States.

Shaibaie, Marie, Director General, Iran Museums, Iran.

Tyazhelov, V., Head of Department, State Pushkin Museum of Fine Arts, Moscow, U.S.S.R.

Westerlund, Stella, Riksutställningar, Stockholm, Sweden.

Select bibliography

Prepared by the Unesco-ICOM Documentation Centre, Paris, in collaboration with Stella Westerlund

1 AGREN, Per-Uno. On the preparation of a new exhibit in the regional museum of Västerbotten (Sweden). *Museum* (Paris, Unesco), Vol. 28, No. 3, 1976, p. 170-175, ill. [Also in French.]

2 ALDERSON, William T.; LOW, Shirley P. *Interpretation of historic sites.* Nashville, Tenn., American Association for State and Local History, 1976. 189 p., ill., bibliogr.

3 ANDERSON, Duane C. Project ETW: an exemplary school-museum program. *Curator* (New York, N.Y.), Vol. 16, No. 2, June 1973, p. 141-157, ill.

4 ARNELL, Ulla *et al.* *Going to exhibitions.* Stockholm, Riksutställningar (Swedish Travelling Exhibitions), 1976. 132 p., ill.

5 ASSOCIATION DES MUSEES DE BELGIQUE. *Programme d'action pour une nouvelle politique des musées.* Bruxelles, 1975. 8 p. [Available from the Belgian National Committee of ICOM.]

6 *L'atelier des enfants hors Beaubourg.* Paris, Centre Georges Pompidou, 1977. [28] p., ill., plan.

7 AVE, Joachim; PATZWALL, Kurt. Arbeitsgruppe Museumspädagogik - Bilanz und Perspektiven. *Neue Museumskunde* (Berlin, German Democratic Republic), Vol. 17, No. 3, 1974, p.202-209, bibliogr.

8 BAY, Ann. *Museum programs for young people. Case studies.* Sponsored by the Smithsonian Institution, with a grant from the National Endowment for the Humanities. Washington, D.C., Smithsonian Institution, 1973. viii, 282 p.

9 BEARDSLEY, Don G. Helping teachers to use museums. *Curator* (New York, N.Y.), Vol. 18, No. 3, September 1975, p. 192-199.

10 BUNNING, Richard L. A perspective on the museum's role in community adult education. *Curator* (New York, N.Y.), Vol. 17, No. 1, March 1974, p. 56-63, bibliogr.

11 BURCH, Glenn E.; ULLAND, Linda M. Learning by living. *Museum News* (Washington, D.C.), Vol. 55, No. 1, September - October 1976, p. 23-31, ill.

12 CELESTE, Maria. A meeting in Rome on the educational role of museums. *Museum* (Paris, Unesco), Vol. 27, No. 3, 1975, p. 147-151, ill. /Also in French./

13 CHASE, Richard A. Museums as learning environments. *Museum News* (Washington, D.C.), Vol. 54, No. 1, September - October 1975, p. 37-43, ill., bibliogr.

14 CHRISTIANSEN, Niels A.; MICHELSEN, F.; TORM, Helge. *Fortidsformidling og fromtidsproblemer*. Holbaek, Naestved og Roskilde Museer, 1977. 64 p., ill.

15 *Communicating with the museum visitor. Guidelines for planning. Prepared by the Communications Design Team of the Royal Ontario Museum, Toronto, Canada, April 1976*. Toronto, The Royal Ontario Museum, 1976. 491 p., ill., bibliogr. (Ia. Section 1, Museum. Part A. Education and Learning, p. 17-24).

16 CONDIT, Louise. Children and art. In : *Museums, imagination and education*, p. 61-82. Paris, Unesco, 1973. 148 p., ill. (Museums and monuments, 15.) /Also in French./

17 Council of Europe. *Report on animation in Sweden with some case-studies*, by Inger Arlemalm. Strasbourg, 1977. 67 p. /Also in French./

18 __________. Council for Cultural Co-operation. *How to visit a museum*, by Pierre Rebetez. Strasbourg, 1970. 188 p., ill., bibliogr. /Also in French./

19 __________. __________. *Le musée, agent d'innovation culturelle*, by Bernard Gilman. Strasbourg, 1977. iv, 38 p.

20 DIXON, Brian ; COURTNEY, Alice ; BAILEY, Robert.

The museum and the Canadian public / Le musée et le public canadien. Toronto, Government of Canada, 1974. 381 p.

21 DUNN, John R. Museum interpretation/education : the need for definition / Le besoin de définir l'interprétation et l'éducation. *Gazette* (Ottawa), Vol. 10, No. 1, Winter 1977, p. 12-16, 60-63.

22 *Education in the art museum. Proceedings of a conference of art museum educators, held in Cleveland, Ohio, November 4 and 5, 1971.* New York, N.Y., The Association of Art Museum Directors, 1972. 85 p., bibliogr.

23 *Education through museums.* A bibliography compiled by G.I. McCabe. London, Group for Educational Services in Museums, 1972. 8 p. Addendum 1975.

24 ELLIOT, Eisner W. *Educating artistic vision.* New York, N.Y., Macmillan, 1972. 306 p., ill., bibliogr.

25 *Enseignants et enseignés. Exposition du Musée de Bretagne, 10 mai - 15 septembre 1977.* Rennes, Musée de Bretagne, 1977. 160 p.

26 *Fare scuola al museo. Dialoghi con i ragazzi delle scuole elementari e medie di Milano sulle opere d'arte.* Milano, Associazione Amici del Poldi Pezzoli, 1976. 71 p.

27 FELTHAM, Heleanor. Education and the small museum. *Kalori* (Sydney), No. 51, May 1976, p. 21-26, ill.

28 FRIEDLÄNDER, Renate. Creative encounter with museums. Experiment of the Cologne Museums Educational Service. *Museum* (Paris, Unesco), Vol. 28, No. 1, 1976, p. 14-27, ill. [Also in French.]

29 GABIANELLI, Vincent J.; MUNYER, Edward A. A place to learn. *Museum News* (Washington, D.C.), Vol. 53, No. 4, December 1974, p. 28-33, ill.

30 GARCÍA, Coral Ordoñez. The Casa del Museo, Mexico City ; an experiment in bringing the museum to the people. *Museum* (Paris, Unesco), Vol. 27, No. 2, 1975, p. 70-77, ill. [Also in French.]

31 GAZEAU, Marie-Thérèse. *L'enfant et le musée.* Préface de Jean Chatelain. Paris, Les Editions ouvrières, 1974. 158 p., bibliogr. (Collection Enfance heureuse)

32 GIRAUDY, Danièle ; BOUILHET, Henri. *Le musée et la vie.* Paris, La Documentation française, 1977. 96 p., ill., bibliogr.

33 GOLDMAN, Katherine J. (ed.). *Opportunities for extending museum contributions to pre-college science education. Summary report of a Conference supported by the National Science Foundation...* Washington, D.C., The Smithsonian Institution, 1970. v, 223 p.

34 GÓMEZ MILLAS, Juan. Museums and lifelong education. *Museum* (Paris, Unesco), Vol. 25, No. 3, 1973, p. 157-164, ill. /Also in French./

35 GORDON, Ayala. Ten years of work in the Youth Wing. *The Israel Museum News* (Jerusalem), No. 11, 1976, p. 27-34, ill.

36 HALE, John. Museums and the teaching of history. *Museum* (Paris, Unesco), Vol. 21, No. 1, 1968, p. 67-72, ill. /Also in French./

37 HAMMOND, Peter. Learning at the Tower. *Museums Journal* (London), Vol. 77, No. 2, September 1977, p. 56-58, ill.

38 *Handbook of programs for museum educators.* Ed. by Allan D. Griesemer. Lincoln, Nebr., Mountain-Plains Museum Conference, 1977. 160 p.

39 *Hands-on-museums : partners in learning. A report from Educational Facilities Laboratories.* New York, N.Y., Educational Facilities Laboratories, 1975. 44 p., ill.

40 HANSEN, Hans Ole. The historical workshop, Denmark : The Lejre Centre. *Museum* (Paris, Unesco), Vol. 27, No. 1, 1975, p. 22-28, ill. /Also in French./

41 HODGE, John. Simulation games : an experiment in museum education. *Kalori* (Sydney), No. 53, December 1977, p. 20-25, ill.

42 HUDSON, Kenneth. Learning stations, customized worksheets and exhibit effectiveness : the new museum jargon. *Museums Journal* (London), Vol. 75, No. 4, March 1976, p. 165-166.

43 ____________. *Museums for the 1980s ; a survey of world trends.* Paris, Unesco; London, Macmillan, 1977. 198 p., ill., bibliogr.

44 International Council of Museums (ICOM). *Training of museum personnel/ La formation du personnel des musées.* Published with the help of the

Smithsonian Institution, Washington, D.C. London, Hugh Evelyn for the International Council of Museums, 1970. 242 p. (Reports and papers on museums, 5)

45 ______. *The museum in the service of man : today and tomorrow. The museum's educational and cultural role... Papers from the 9th General Conference of ICOM, Paris and Grenoble, August - September 1971/Le musée au service des hommes d'aujourd'hui et de demain. Le rôle éducatif et culturel du musée... Actes de la 9e Conférence générale de l'ICOM, Paris et Grenoble, août - septembre 1971.* Paris, ICOM, 1972. 195 p., ill.

46 ______. The Australian National Committee for ICOM. *Museum contributions to education. First Australian ICOM Seminar, Melbourne, 1971.* 142 p., ill.

47 ______. Working Party on Kits. *Kit, What is that?* Stockholm, Riksutställningar, 1973. 25 p., ill. /In English, French, Spanish, German and Russian./

48 *ICOM Education* (Former *Museums' Annual/Annales des musées*). Gudrun V. Hård and CECA (ICOM International Committee for Education and Cultural Action) (eds). Stockholm, Riksutställningar, No. 7, 1975-1976. 65 p., ill., bibliogr.

49 ______. Stockholm, Riksutställningar, No. 8, 1977-1978. /In press./

50 *Indagine sulla didattica dei beni culturali in Lombardia.* Milano, Unicopli /for the/ Centro fra ricercatori per i beni culturali in Lombardia, 1977. 444 p., ill.

51 *Internationales Seminar "Kommunikations- und Lernfeld Museum", Ingelheim, 17-19 Oktober 1977.* Köln, Deutsche Unesco-Kommission, 1977. /79/ p.

52 JELINEK, Jan. The modern, living museum. *Museum* (Paris, Unesco), Vol. 27, No. 2, 1975, p. 52-59, ill. /Also in French./

53 JOR, Finn. *The demystification of culture : animation and creativity. A survey commissioned by the Council for Cultural Co-operation.* Oslo, Council of Europe Conference of Ministers with Responsibility for Cultural Affairs, 1976. 122 p., ill.

54 *Khudozhestvennye muzei i esteticheskoe vospitanie trudyashchikhsya* /Art museums and the aesthetic education of the workers/. Moskva, 1974.

55 Kindermalhaus. *Arbeit mit Kindern im Kunstmuseum Düsseldorf. Eine Dokumentation.* Düsseldorf, Kunstmuseum Düsseldorf, 1974. 160 p., ill.

56 KURYLO, Lynne. On the need for a theory of museum learning. *Gazette* (Ottawa, CMA/AMC), Vol. 9, No. 3, 1976, p. 20-24, ill., bibliogr.

57 LARIONOVA, E. The aesthetic education of children in the museum. (Tr. from Russian.) *Museum* (Paris, Unesco), Vol. 21, No. 1, 1968, p. 45-47, ill. /Also in French./

58 LARRAURI, Iker. The school museum programme in Mexico. *Museum* (Paris, Unesco), Vol. 27, No. 2, 1975, p. 60-69, ill. /Also in French./

59 LEE, Sherman E. Art museum and education. *Art International* (Lugano), Vol. 21, No. 1, 1977, p. 48-51.

60 LOAR, Peggy A. The arts and the three Rs. A look at the potential of state plans that would integrate the arts into the public school curriculum. *Museum News* (Washington, D.C.), Vol. 55, No. 1, September - October 1976, p. 43-47, ill.

61 LUCA, Mark. The museum as educator ; annotated bibliography of the growth of an idea. In : *Museums, imagination and education*, p. 145-148. Paris, Unesco, 1973. 148 p., ill. (Museums and monuments, 15.) /Also in French./

62 MADEJA, Stanley S. *All the arts for every child. Final report on the arts in general education project in the school district of University City, Mo.* New York, N.Y., The John D. Rockefeller 3rd Fund, Inc., 1973. 111 p., ill.

63 MARCOUSÉ, Renée. Changing museums in a changing world. In : *Museums, imagination and education*, p. 17-21. Paris, Unesco, 1973. 148 p., ill. (Museums and monuments, 15.) /Also in French./

64 ____________. *Using objects. Visual learning and visual awareness in the museum and the classroom.* London, 1974. 158 p., ill.

65 MATTHAI, Robert A. ; DEAVER, Neil E. Child-centered learning. *Museum News* (Washington, D.C.), Vol. 54, No. 4, March - April 1976, p. 15-19, ill., bibliogr.

66 *Measuring the immeasurable : a pilot study of*

museum effectiveness, by Minda Borum..., *sponsored by the Association of Science-Technology Centers (ASTC)*... Washington, D.C., ASTC, 1977. xvi, 114 p.

67 MESALLAM, Mahmoud Hassan. The exhibitions a developing country needs. In : *Museums, imagination and education*, p. 113-122. Paris, Unesco, 1973. 148 p., ill. (Museums and monuments, 15.) /Also in French./

68 Le musée et les jeunes. *Clés pour les arts* (Bruxelles), No. 22, June 1972. 31 p., ill.

69 *Le musée, l'enfant et son milieu quotidien.* Bordeaux, Musée d'Aquitaine, 1974. 84 p., ill. (Documents d'animation pédagogique et socio-culturelle, 1.)

70 Die Museen und die kulturellästhetische Bildung und Erziehung der Schuljugend. *Schule und Museum im einheitlichen sozialistischen Bildungssystem der DDR* (Berlin, German Democratic Republic, Arbeitsgruppe Museumspädagogik), No. 10, 1975. 100 p.

71 Musées et jeunes d'âge scolaire. *Musées et collections publiques de France* (Paris), Vol. 111, No. 2, 1970, suppl. 64 p.

72 /Museum accessibility to the handicapped/. *Museum News* (Washington, D.C.), Vol. 55, No. 3, January - February 1977, p. 15-31, 45.

73 The museum and its visitors. In : HUDSON, Kenneth. *Museums for the 1980s ; a survey of world trends*, p. 77-145. Paris, Unesco; London, Macmillan, 1977.

74 Museum educators : what are they fighting for ? *Museum News* (Washington, D.C.), Vol. 52, No. 7, April 1974, p. 10-47, ill.

75 *A museum for the people ; a report of proceedings at the Seminar on Neighborhood Museums, held November 20, 21 and 22 1969 at MUSE, Brooklyn, New York.* Ed. by E.D. Harvey and B. Friedberg. New York, N.Y., Arno Press, 1971. 86 p., ill.

76 *Das Museum. Lernort contra Museumtempel.* Ed. by Ellen Spickernagel and Brigitte Walbe. Giessen, Arabas-Verlag, 1976. 179 p., ill. (Special issue of "Kritische Berichte")

77 "Museum und Schule". *Kunst + Unterricht* (Velber bei Hannover), special issue, 1976. 112 p., ill., bibliogr.

78 *Museums and handicapped students. Guidelines for educators.* Washington, D.C., Smithsonian Institution, 1977. xii, 163 p., ill., bibliogr.
79 *Museums and the handicapped. Seminar... College Hall, Leicester, 12-14 September 1975.* Leicester, Leicestershire Museums, Art Galleries and Records Service /for the/ Group for Educational Services in Museums, 1976. 68 p., ill., bibliogr.
80 *Museums and the environment : a handbook for education...* Ed. by Ruth Norton Oliver. Washington, D.C., American Association of Museums, 1971. 261 p., ill.
81 *Museums' Annual/Annales des musées.* Renée Marcousé (ed). Oxford, ICOM, No. 1-6, 1964-1969. (Cont. *ICOM Education*)
82 *Museums in education.* London, HMSO, 1971. 56 p., ill. (Education Survey, 12)
83 *Museums in South, Southeast and East Asia ; review and report, ICOM Regional Agency in Asia 1967-1977,* by Grace Morley. New Delhi, ICOM Regional Agency in Asia, 1977. 22 p.
84 Museumspädagogik. *Berliner Museen* (Berlin, West), ser. 3, 1975, suppl., p. 1-16, ill.
85 *Museumspädagogik. Museen als Bildungsstätten* /by/ Wolfgang Klausewitz. Frankfurt/Main, Deutscher Museumsbund, 1975. 191 p., ill.
86 Muzea w procesie wychowania młodziezy /Museums in the process of youth education/. Ed. by Krzysztof Nowinski. *Biblioteka muzealnictwa i ochrony zabytków* (Warszawa), s. B, Vol. 46, 1977. 166 p.
87 NEWSON, Barbara ; SILVER, Adele Z. (eds). *The art museum as educator.* Berkeley, Calif., University of California Press, 1977. 800 p., ill.
88 NEWTON, Earle W. Cultural institutions as learning resources. *Curator* (New York, N.Y.), Vol. 17, No. 3, September 1974, p. 225-230.
89 Numéro spécial consacré au Service d'animation pédagogique et d'action culturelle au Muséum national d'histoire naturelle. *Bulletin de liaison des musées d'histoire naturelle* (Paris), No. 34, April 1978, p. 2-35.
90 OLOFSSON, Ulla Keding. Temporary and travelling exhibitions. In : *Museums, imagination and education,* p. 91-103. Paris, Unesco,

1973. 148 p., ill. (Museums and monuments, 15.) /Also in French./

91 ___________. The role of the museum in a decentralized cultural policy. Meeting of the International Committee of ICOM for Education and Cultural Action, Umeå, 1976. *Museum* (Paris, Unesco), Vol. 29, No. 1, 1977, p. 52-55, ill. /Also in French./

92 OPRIS, Ioan. Muzeul si scoala. Metode si forme de colaborare. *Revista muzeelor si monumentelor, muzee* (Bucureşti), Vol. 14, No. 9, 1977, p. 43-45.

93 *Out and about. A teacher's guide to safety on educational visits.* London, Evans/Methuen Educational for the Schools Council, 1972. 100 p., ill., bibliogr.

94 PATZWALL, Kurt. *Schatzkammer aufschliessen.* Berlin, German Democratic Republic, Volk und Wissen, 1973. 64 p., ill. (Series "Elternhaus und Schule")

95 ___________; EHRLICH, Willi. *Wir besuchen ein Museum. Handreichungen zur Bildung und Erziehung im Museum für Leiter von Gruppen.* Berlin German Democratic Republic, Volk und Wissen, 1976. 243 p., ill., bibliogr.

96 PELTIER SAN PEDRO, Rodolfo. INAH's local and school museums program. In : Mavis Bryant (ed). *Museums of Mexico and the United States : policies and problems. Papers from two conferences, San Antonio, Texas, October 1976, Mexico City, December 1976*, p. 19-27. Austin, Texas Historical Foundation, 1977.

97 PIEROTTI, Ray. Be...see...touch...respond. *Museum News* (Washington, D.C.), Vol. 52, No. 4, December 1973, p. 43-48, ill.

98 PINNA, Giovanni. Creation of a fossil museum at Besano, Italy ; community initiative. *Museum* (Paris, Unesco), Vol. 28, No. 1, 1976, p. 3-7, ill. /Also in French./

99 PITMAN-GELLES, Bonnie. Pumpkins into coaches : youth education in museums. /not yet published/

100 PRAKASH, Satya. Education through art museums - a review. *Journal of Indian Museums* (New Delhi), Vol. 27-28, 1971-1972, p. 15-26.

101 *Die Praxis der Museumsdidaktik. Bericht über ein internationales Seminar der Deutschen UNESCO-Kommission, Museum Folkwang, November 1971, in*

Essen. Köln, Deutsche UNESCO-Kommission; Pullach-München, Verlag Dokumentation, 1974. 171 p.

102 PROCTOR, D.V. Museums - teachers, students, children. In : *Museums, imagination and education*, p. 23-29. Paris, Unesco, 1973. 148 p., ill. (Museums and monuments, 15.) /Also in French./

103 *Pterodactyls and old lace. Museums in education.* London, Evans/Methuen Educational for the Schools Council, 1972. 95 p., ill.

104 RAZGON, Abraham. Museums and multidisciplinary universal education in the USSR. *Museum* (Paris, Unesco), Vol. 28, No. 1, 1976, p. 28-33, ill. /Also in French./

105 READ, John. Television and the museum. In : *Museums, imagination and education*, p. 83-90. Paris, Unesco, 1973. 148 p., ill. (Museums and monuments, 15.) /Also in French./

106 REQUE, Barbara. From object to idea. /By adopting the techniques of reading comprehension, museums can enable teachers and students to become independent "readers" of museum objects./ *Museum News* (Washington, D.C.), Vol. 56, No. 3, January - February 1978, p. 45-47, ill.

107 ROHMEDER, Jürgen. *Methoden und Medien der Museumsarbeit. Pädagogische Betreuung der Einzelbesucher im Museum, mit Karikaturen von Marie Marcks.* Köln, DuMont Buchverlag, 1977. 160 p., ill.

108 *Rol' khudozhestvennykh muzeev v esteticheskom vospitanii shkol'nikov. Nauchnyĭ seminar. Chasti I i II.* /The role of art museums in the aesthetic education of schoolchildren ; Scientific Seminar. Parts I and II./. Moskva, 1973.

109 Le rôle éducatif des musées. *Vie des musées 76; Bulletin des Musées de Wallonie et de Bruxelles* (Bruxelles), 1976, p. 14-74, ill.

110 *The role of museums in adult education for development. Unesco Symposium organized by ICOM, Malacca - Kuala Lumpur, December 14-18, 1972.* New Delhi, ICOM Regional Agency, 1973. 34 p.

111 *Selective bibliography of research on museum audiences, exhibit effectiveness and visitor behavior.* Prepared by the Working Party on Research of CECA (ICOM International Committee on Education and Cultural Action) and C.G. Screven, 1977. 14p., multigr.

112 *Sezione didattica della Galleria degli Uffizi. Metodi, programmi, strutture, 1970-1975*, by Maria Fossi Todorow and Barbara Cinelli. Firenze, Saprintendenza alle Gallerie, 1975. 31 p., ill.

113 SHETTEL, Harris H. Exhibits : art form or educational medium? *Museum News* (Washington, D.C.), Vol. 52, No. 1, September 1973, p. 32-41, ill., bibliogr.

114 SUBRAMANIAN, R. Science, museums and planetaria. In : *Museums, imagination and education*, p. 43-60. Paris, Unesco, 1973. 148 p., ill. (Museums and monuments, 15.) [Also in French.]

115 *Survey of education programs at science-technology centers.* Comp. by Kay Davis. Ed. by Lee Kimche. Washington, D.C., ASTC, 1976. 68 p., ill.

116 SZPAKOWSKI, André. Collaboration between museum and school. In : *Museums, imagination and education,* p. 133-143. Paris, Unesco, 1973. 148 p., ill. (Museums and monuments, 15.) [Also in French.]

117 TAYLOR, Anne P. Children and artifacts - a replacement for textbook learning. *Curator* (New York, N.Y.), Vol. 16, No. 1, March 1973, p. 25-29.

118 THIER, Herbert D.; LINN, Marcia C. The value of interactive learning experiences. *Curator* (New York, N.Y.), Vol. 19, No. 3, September 1976, p. 233-245, ill., bibliogr.

119 THOMAS, W. Stephen. How do museums use the mass media? A report from the United States. In : *Museums, imagination and education,* p. 123-131. Paris, Unesco, 1973. 148 p., ill. (Museums and monuments, 15.) [Also in French.]

120 TIBONE, Maria Luisa. *Il museo, un incontro nuovo.* Torino, Paravia, 1977. 64 p., ill. (Ideechiave, 14.)

121 TOUCET, P. An economic role for museums in the developing countries. In : *Museums, imagination and education,* p. 31-42. Paris, Unesco, 1973. 148 p., ill. (Museums and monuments, 15.) [Also in French.]

122 Unesco. Musées, société, connaissances / Museums, society, knowledge. *Cahiers d'histoire mondiale /*

Journal of world history (Paris, Unesco ; Neuchâtel, Editions de la Baconnière), Vol. 14, No. 1, 1972. 204 p., ill., bibliogr.

123 ____________. *Museums, imagination and education.* Paris, 1973. 148 p., ill. (Museums and monuments, 15.) /Also in French./ (Italian translation : Musei Società Educazione. Guide per operatori culturali. Roma, Armando, 1976.)

124 VANDERWAY, Richard. Planning museum tours : for school groups. *History News* (Nashville, Tenn., American Association for State and Local History), Vol. 32, No. 3, March 1977, 12 p., ill., bibliogr. (Technical leaflet, 93)

125 VARINE-BOHAN, Hugues de. The modern museum : requirements and problems of a new approach. *Museum* (Paris, Unesco), Vol. 28, No. 3, 1976, p. 130-143. /Also in French./

126 VIGTEL, Gudmund. Child's work. *Museum News* (Washington, D.C.), Vol. 55, No. 1, September - October 1976, p. 32-35, ill.

127 VILENSKAYA, K.; AGAFOSHINA, B. Reaching a distant public. In : *Museums, imagination and education,* p. 105-111. Paris, Unesco, 1973. 148 p., ill. (Museums and monuments, 15.) /Also in French./

128 WASHBURN, Wilcomb E. Do museums educate? *Curator* (New York, N.Y.), Vol. 18, No. 3, September 1975, p. 211-218, bibliogr.

129 WATERMAN, Stafford M. Museums as educational partners. *AGMANZ News* (Auckland), Vol. 8, No. 2, May 1977, p. 21-24.

130 WEISBERG, Gabriel P. On the importance of museum education. *La Chronique des arts* (Paris), No. 1276-1277, May - June 1975, p. 1-3.

131 WENGEN, G.D. van. *Educatief werk in musea.* Groningen, H.D. Tjeenk Willink, 1975. 109 p. (Vormingswerk, theorie & praktijk, 17)

132 WITTLIN, A.S. *Museums, in search of a usable future.* Cambridge, Mass., M.I.T. Press, 1970. 300 p., ill.

133 WOHLER, J. Patrick. *The history museum as an effective educational institution.* Ottawa, National Museums of Canada, 1976. 80 p., bibliogr. (National Museum of Man Mercury Series, Communications Division Paper, 4.)

134 YOUNGPETER, John M. Museum field trips - enhancement through creative planning. *Curator* (New York, N.Y.), Vol. 16, No. 3, September 1973, p. 267-270.

135 ZENTS, Ye. Prosvetitel'naya rabota khudozhestvennykh muzeev (1918-1923) /The educational work of art museums (1918-1923)/. *Iskusstvo* /Art/, No. 2, 1968, p. 34-36.

136 ZETTERBERG, Hans. *Museums and adult education.* London, Evelyn, Adams & Mackay for the International Council of Museums, 1968. 89 p., ill., bibliogr. (Reports and papers on museums, 4.) /Also in French./

137 ZILVER, Adele Z. Education in a museum : a conservative adventure. *Curator* (New York, N.Y.), Vol. 15, No. 1, 1972, p. 72-85, ill.

138 Zur Theorie und Methodik der Bildung und Erziehung im Museum /by/ Karl-Heinz Tomaschewsky, Werner Salzwedel, Kurt Patzwall /et al./. *Schule und Museum* (Berlin, West), Vol. 11, 1976, p. 3-54, bibliogr.

(B.30) ED.78/XVI-10/A